Beirut

Jessica Lee

Credits

Footprint credits

Editor: Alan Murphy
Production and layout: Angus Dawson,
Emma Bryers
Maps: Kevin Feeney

Managing Director: Andy Riddle
Commercial Director: Patrick Dawson
Publisher: Alan Murphy
Publishing Managers: Felicity Laughton,
Nicola Gibbs.
Digital Editors: Jo Williams,
Tom Mellors
Marketing and PR: Liz Harper
Sales: Diane McEntee
Advertising: Renu Sibal
Finance and Administration:
Elizabeth Taylor

Photography credits

Front cover: Khatam Al Anbija Mosque,
diak/Shutterstock
Back cover: Pigeon rocks, Ryan Rodrick
Beiler/Shutterstock

Printed and bound in the United States
of America

Every effort has been made to ensure that
the facts in this guidebook are accurate.
However, travellers should still obtain advice
from consulates, airlines, etc about travel
and visa requirements before travelling.
The authors and publishers cannot
accept responsibility for any loss, injury or
inconvenience however caused.

Publishing information

Footprint *Focus Beirut*
1st edition
© Footprint Handbooks Ltd
July 2011

ISBN: 978 1 908206 11 4
CIP DATA: A catalogue record for this book is
available from the British Library

® Footprint Handbooks and the Footprint
mark are a registered trademark of Footprint
Handbooks Ltd

Published by Footprint
6 Riverside Court
Lower Bristol Road
Bath BA2 3DZ, UK
T +44 (0)1225 469141
F +44 (0)1225 469461
footprinttravelguides.com

Distributed in the USA by Globe Pequot
Press, Guilford, Connecticut

The content of Footprint *Focus Beirut*
has been taken directly from Footprint's
Lebanon Handbook which was researched
and written by Jessica Lee.

Contents

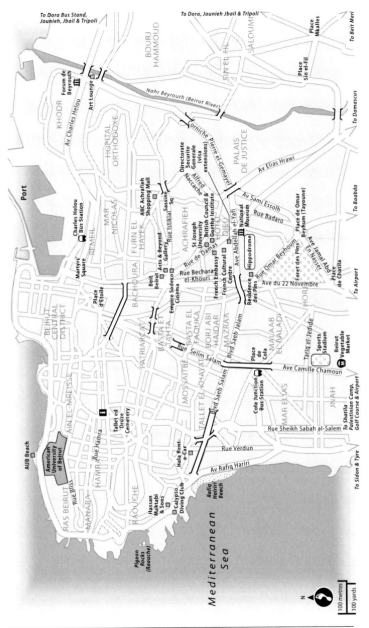

Battered and bruised she may be but Beirut refuses to lie down and play dead. This capital is a chameleon of many faces where trendy bars and glitzy restaurants sit side by side with bullet-ridden and gutted building shells; where the polish and sparkle of the new Downtown district, complete with designer-clad and botoxed shoppers, sits in stark contrast to the Dahiya – the sprawling working-class suburbs which make up the southern section of the city. Beirut, still wearing the scars of war on its sleeve, is the Arab world at its most cosmopolitan and is a proud emblem for Lebanon's remarkable recovery and survival after years of turmoil.

Although much of Beirut's rich history has been obliterated by a succession of natural disasters, invasion and war, there are still vestiges of the past to be found. Peel back the flashy exterior and peeping out from the shadows of the high rises you'll find sedately beautiful and crumbling neo-Ottoman buildings that have, as yet, escaped the developer's demolition ball. The National Museum, although small, is an excellent showcase of Lebanon's antiquities, and among Downtown's pristine streets small pockets of Roman-era ruins, unearthed during the post-civil war development, have been preserved, giving visitors a taste of Beirut's importance throughout the ages.

Rising sharply from the coastal plain, the Mount Lebanon range is home to some of the most spectacular and varied scenery in the country, if not in the entire Middle East. The landscape here is simply awesome, with peaks averaging around 2000 m and rising to 3083 m at the summit of Qornet es-Saouda. A particular highlight is the Qadisha Valley in the north, which offers a wealth of hiking opportunities amid jaw-dropping scenery.

Planning your trip

When to go

Lebanon's climate is at its most attractive during spring and autumn, though its unique topography and long Mediterranean seaboard mean that there are enormous local variations in any given season. Choosing a 'best time' depends entirely on where you are planning to go and what you are planning to do.

The **coast** gets very hot and humid during the summer months (mid-May to mid-September) and particularly so during July and August. Visiting Beirut or towns along the coast is hard work in these conditions and this is also when the beach resorts are at their busiest. Both spring and autumn are short-lived, but during March, April and October there are usually spells of pleasantly warm and reasonably dry weather. Note, however, that March/April is also the time of the *khamsin*, when hot, dry, sand-laden winds sometimes blow in from the Sahara. Winters on the coast are cool and rainy, with frequent heavy thunderstorms and rough seas.

The **mountains** enjoy an essentially alpine climate. The summer months see the Lebanese decamping to the mountains in droves, exchanging the heat and humidity on the coast for blissfully cool mountain breezes and warm sunny days. The cooling effects of the breezes do not reduce the burning power of the sun, however, and proper protection is essential. Higher up, it gets quite chilly at night, even in July and August. Though temperatures get steadily cooler, the weather generally stays pleasantly dry and sunny right through to November. By December it is cold and the winter rains and snows begin in earnest, usually lasting through to around May, when it begins to warm up again.

Getting there

Air

All international flights into Lebanon arrive at **Rafiq Hariri International Airport**, 9 km south of central Beirut. See page 22.

Flights from the UK Both Lebanon's national airline **Middle East Airlines (MEA)** (www. mea.com.lb) and BMI (www.flybmi.com) have daily direct flights to Beirut. Prices start from around £400 return but can rise during the peak holiday period of June to August, and at Christmas.

Flights from the rest of Europe MEA (www.mea.com.lb) has daily direct flights from **Paris, Frankfurt, Geneva, Larnaca** and **Athens**, and several flights per week from **Rome, Milan** and **Nice** throughout the year. During the peak holiday period of May to September they also fly from **Brussels, Copenhagen** and **Berlin**. Return flight prices start from €450 but there is generally a price hike during the June to August summer season. Throughout the year look out for MEA's very good promotional deals, which advertise return flights from European destinations for as little as €250.

Other European airlines that fly into Beirut include: from Paris, **Air France** (www. airfrance.fr); from Frankfurt, **Lufthansa** (www.lufthansa.com); from Athens, **Olympic** (www.olympicairlines.com); from Larnaca, **Cyprus Airways** (www.cyprusair.com.cy); and from Rome **Alitalia** (www.alitalia.it).

Flights from North America There are no direct flights from North America. The cheapest option is to fly into London or Paris and book an onward flight from there. The quickest (though not necessarily the cheapest) option is to book through **MEA** (www.mea.com.lb) who, in conjunction with **Air France** (www.airfrance.fr), have daily flights from several North American cities with a quick stopover in Paris' Charles De Gaulle Airport to change planes. Return flights cost from around US$1600. If you shop around you should be able to find a cheaper deal.

There is also the option of flying first into another nearby country and booking an onward flight to Lebanon from there. **Cairo** (Egypt), **Istanbul** (Turkey), **Amman** (Jordan), **Dubai** (UAE) and **Abu Dhabi** (UAE) all have daily direct flights to Beirut with **MEA** and there are often good deals on other local airlines. For example, **Flydubai** (www.flydubai.com) often has flights from Dubai to Beirut for as little as US$100 while from Istanbul **Pegasus Airlines** (www.flypgs.com) are now offering flights to Beirut starting from US$90.

Flights from Australia and New Zealand Because of the large numbers of Lebanese people living in Australia, there are several airlines that fly to Beirut from Sydney and Melbourne, including **Emirates** (www.emirates.com), **Etihad** (www.etihadairways.com) and **Malaysia Airlines** (www.malaysiaairlines.com). Return flights start from about AUD$2000. All these flights include a stopover at the airline carrier's national hub.

There are no direct flights from New Zealand; either go first to Australia, or else head for Europe or a city in the region, such as **Amman**, **Cairo** or **Istanbul**, and pick up a flight from there.

Getting around

Road

Public transport within Lebanon is cheap, with minibus/bus fares between towns rarely rising above 4000 LBP. Privately operated **minibuses/buses** ply the major routes between towns with Beirut being the central hub. The northern Beirut–Tripoli highway and the southern Beirut–Tyre highway are particularly well connected, as is the route up to Baalbek via the Beirut–Damascus highway. The only route that has frequent air-conditioned coach-style buses is between Beirut and Tripoli; on all other routes expect a selection of squashy minibuses and beaten-up buses (which often don't have air conditioning).

Service taxis (shared taxis), for routes between towns, used to be a lot more prevalent but over the past few years have slowly been replaced by buses and minibuses. They are still useful chiefly for journeys to the south from Beirut.

In more rural areas if you've got a bit of patience and some time up your sleeve you should be able to get to most of the smaller towns using public transport. However, for certain areas, particularly in the Chouf and Mount Lebanon, you'll find public transport options either extremely infrequent or non-existent. If you want to explore areas such as the Jebel Tannourine and the Adonis Valley you really need to hire a car or driver.

Car With your own vehicle you have far greater freedom to explore more out-of-the-way places and to stop wherever you choose. The type of vehicle you select, whether it be a van/campervan, car or motorbike, depends very much on your own personal preferences and needs. Overlanding through the Middle East does not require a vehicle that's been specially modified in any way (unless, of course, you are planning to head down into Africa), although the vehicle should obviously be in excellent mechanical condition before you set off.

Hiring a car in Lebanon is comparatively cheap, with rates starting from around US$40 per day for the smallest cars. During peak periods (May, August-September and December), it is extremely difficult to lay your hands on the cheapest hire cars; if possible, bookings should be made at least two weeks in advance. Even outside these times, you are advised to book at least a week ahead. On all but the cheapest deals, you can usually get discounts for periods of a week or more.

If you want to be able to visit more remote areas of the country at will, particularly in the mountains, hiring a car is the only really viable option (short of hitching or hiring a taxi for the day) unless you have your own vehicle. Beirut is the main centre for car hire, with numerous companies offering everything from small hatchbacks to luxury Mercedes and 4WD.

Conditions vary from company to company. A full driving licence held for at least two years is required by all. Minimum ages vary from 21-25. All require a deposit, either in the form of a credit card imprint, or else cash in the region of US$500. Be sure to check whether the quoted rates include unlimited mileage (this is usually the case for all rentals of three days or more or, in some cases, one week or more).

Insurance arrangements in Lebanon are, in general, reliable (although policies carry a somewhat alarming clause along the lines of "war, invasion and hold-up are not covered"). However, being involved in an accident (even if it is only a low-speed knock in heavy traffic), or having your car stolen, are infinitely more likely scenarios. In either case, you are liable for an excess of anywhere between US$300 (for minor damage to a small car) and US$2500 (for theft or a total write-off of a luxury car).

Most companies offer CDW (Crash Damage Waiver) as an optional extra (usually between US$5-10 per day depending on the type of car); this reduces (but does not completely remove) the excess payable in the event of an accident. Also worth considering is PAI (Personal Accident Insurance), usually costing an additional US$3 per day. Many of the big international car hire companies in Lebanon automatically include CDW in the cost of their hire. Whatever you do, make sure you read the small print before hiring a car. However carefully you drive, there is always the risk of an accident, but the risk of theft can be greatly reduced by always engaging the steering lock and by making use of supervised parking lots in towns and cities.

Avis (www.avis.com.lb), **Budget** (www.budget-rental.com), and **Hertz** (www.hertz.com) all have offices in Beirut, while **Europcar** is represented by **Lenacar** (www.lenacar.com). The main international rental firms all have very similar prices. **Europcar/Lenacar** offers small cars (such as a Renault Clio) with unlimited mileage from US$40 per day. For the same time period a medium-sized car (Peugeot 206 or similar) is US$50 per day and a larger car (such as a Nissan Sunny) starts from US$55 per day. They also do special deals for weekend hire (from Friday afternoon to Monday morning, small car hire costs US$92).

Hitching On any of the major transport routes, hitching is more or less impossible simply because as soon as you stick your thumb out you will attract the attention of any passing service taxi or minibus driver. However, on quiet roads in remote areas hitching is possible and may be your only form of transport. Remember that hitching in the Western sense (for a free ride) is a foreign concept here. Hitching takes place because there is a limited (or non-existent) public transport system in the area, and you should always offer to pay the driver who picked you up. For women travellers, hitching alone can never be recommended.

Sleeping

The main towns and tourist centres nearly all have a decent amount of accommodation options, though Beirut definitely has the most choice.

There are numerous top-end hotels in and around the capital and most of the international chains are represented. The capital has an excellent selection of mid-range options, while outside Beirut more and more guesthouses and B&Bs have opened up. It's worth noting that outside of the peak summer season many of the top-end hotels often offer huge discounts (sometimes as much as 50% off the quoted price), putting them into the mid-range price bracket. Lebanon doesn't have the same range of budget choices as Egypt or Syria but the accommodation scene in this price bracket is improving, particularly in Beirut and in tourist centres such as Tripoli, Bcharre and Baalbek.

DHIAFEE hotel network

Traditionally most tourists to Lebanon have stayed in Beirut and only ventured out to the rest of the country on day trips. The DHIAFEE hotel network was set up to reverse this trend; helping to spread the benefits of the tourism dollar throughout the country by promoting accommodation options all over Lebanon. Options range from small family-run hotels and simple guesthouses where there may only be a couple of rooms, to youth hostel-style accommodation and religious lodgings in local monasteries. All are in the mid-range to budget price categories. The best of DHIAFEE's accommodation options have been listed in this book, but for a full list go to www.dhiafeeprogram.org.

Camping

There is a good campsite at Amchit, a couple of kilometeres to the north of Byblos. It's a well-run, friendly place that offers chalets and 'tungalows' (tent-like bungalows), as well as camping. In the Lebanon mountains, above Afqa, there is another good camping option offering full facilities as well as a wide range of outdoor activities. There are a couple of other camping options, though they are usually very primitive. In small towns, many of the hotels will allow you to pitch a tent if you ask. If you want to free camp in rural areas you are strongly advised to ask for permission before setting up camp. Free camping in the Bekaa Valley and in the south is not really advisable as the military are likely to be rather touchy.

Eating and drinking

Food

Lebanon has a well deserved reputation for the best cooking in the region and it is here that you'll get a true taste of what Arabic cuisine is really about. The fusing of Arabic and Mediterranean influences combined with the Lebanese love of food has ensured that eating is always something of a gourmet experience.

Meat, in the form of lamb or chicken, features fairly prominently in the Arab diet, along with staples such as chickpeas (in the form of falafel or hummus), other vegetables, and, of course, bread (*khubz*). Despite the prominence of meat, **vegetarians** can be sure of a nutritious and reasonably varied diet (hummus, falafel, *baba ganoush* and other meze dishes, as well as *fuul*, *fatteh*, salads, rice, vegetable stews and bread).

Beirut and its environs have the highest concentration of restaurants, with everything from cheap snack places and Western-style fast-food joints to sumptuously elegant

Sleeping and eating price codes

Sleeping

$$$$ over US$150 $$$ US$76-150 $$ US$50-75
$ under US$50

Prices include taxes and service charge, but not meals. They are based on a double room, except in the $ range, where prices are almost always per person.

Eating

¶¶¶ over US$12   ¶¶ US$6-12   ¶ under US$6

Prices refer to the cost of a two-course meal for one person, excluding drinks or service charge.

gourmet establishments, with prices to match. Up in the mountains you can often find more traditional places serving excellent meze at very good prices. One place particularly famous for its meze is Zahle, in the Bekaa Valley.

Seafood is considered a particular speciality in Lebanon, probably at least partly because it is so scarce; during the civil war many people took to dynamiting the fish out of the sea and stocks are still seriously depleted. One of the best places for seafood is Tyre, where many of the restaurants specialize in it.

Unlike in neighbouring Syria, food is expensive here and if you're on a tight budget sit-down meals at proper restaurants are more or less out of the question unless you want to splurge.

Drink

Coffee, in its traditional Arabic form, is more widely drunk than **tea**, although in the traditional cafés of Tripoli or Sidon both are popular (the latter usually being brewed from a Lipton's tea bag and served in the Arabic way, black and sweet). In the classy and fashionable cafés of the cities you'll also find the very best espresso, cappuccino and probably every conceivable blend of tea.

Alcohol is readily available and Lebanon has a small but well-regarded wine industry, with the Bekaa Valley vineyards of Ksara, Kefraya and Chateau Musar producing some excellent wines as well as the powerful spirit *arak* (the much-loved Arab aniseed liqueur). There are plenty of locally brewed and imported beers. Almaaza is a good-quality, light lager brewed locally under licence from Amstel. Many places now have draught beers on tap, while a few British-style 'pubs' even have draught Guinness on tap.

Responsible tourism and cultural sensitivities

Clothing

On the surface, Lebanon seems much more relaxed about dress codes than neighbouring Arab countries, and if you've been travelling through the Middle East for a while the sight of the fashionistas of Beirut dressed in the latest body-hugging and cleavage-enhancing fashions can come as something of a shock. In the capital and other cosmopolitan areas (such as **Jounieh**, **Byblos** and most of the rest of the northern coastline, much of **Mount Lebanon** and the **Chouf**, and **Zahle**) you can basically dress as you like. It's important to remember though, that as soon as you travel away from these areas these liberal attitudes do not apply. As soon as you head into more remote, rural and particularly Muslim areas (such as much of the **South** and the **Bekaa Valley**, and centres such as **Tripoli**), attitudes are much more conservative.

The thing to remember when dressing for conservative areas is that shoulders and knees (and everything in between) should be covered. This rule applies to men as well as women. It is also worth noting that the Lebanese place a huge amount of importance on smartness and cleanliness and making the effort to be presentable in public will earn you greater respect wherever you are in the country. See also 'visiting mosques' below.

Conduct
The Lebanese are generally very open and welcoming and will often go out of their way to help foreigners. Return the gesture by being equally polite and friendly.

In traditional Muslim culture it is not usual for a man and woman to shake hands when meeting. Instead place your right hand across your heart, which can also be used as a sign of thank you. In traditional areas open displays of affection between couples are not acceptable in public and can cause great offence. Conversely, it is completely normal for friends of the same sex (male and female) to hold hands and link arms in public.

While eating a shared meal, such as meze, it's acceptable to use your left hand to tear bread but the right hand should be used to take from the communal bowls and also to pass things to people. Always tuck your feet in towards you when sitting down. Feet are considered unclean and it's very rude to point them at someone. Also, crossing your legs while seated is considered rude by some more conservative people.

If you're interested in Lebanon's modern history you're in luck as nearly every Lebanese you will meet is more than happy to talk endlessly about all aspects of local and regional politics. If you find yourself on the receiving end of particularly extreme views, bear in mind that these are people who have lived through some pretty horrific experiences and feelings often run very deep. Note that a great deal of discretion (or better still outright silence) is in order on the subject of visiting Israel.

Visiting mosques Non-Muslims are welcome in most mosques, although in some Shiite mosques they are only allowed into the courtyard and not the prayer hall itself. In any case, always seek permission before entering. Remember that shoes must be removed before entering the prayer hall, although socks can be left on. It is very important that both men and women dress modestly – cover arms and legs (shorts are not acceptable) and, in the case of women, wear a headscarf. At larger, more important mosques, women may be required to hire a full-length black hooded robe at the entrance (and men also if they attempt to enter in shorts).

Essentials A-Z

Accident and emergency
Ambulance: T140. **Fire**: T175. **Police**: T112. **Tourist complaints**: T1735. In the event of an accident an official police/medical report is required for insurance claims.

Bargaining
Lebanon doesn't have as much scope for brushing up on your bargaining skills as other Arab countries, which will come as a relief to some. Many of the souvenir/handicraft stores are fixed price and it will only be in the souqs of Tripoli and Sidon where you may need to put your haggling hat on.

Electricity
220 volts, 50 AC. European 2-pin sockets are the norm.

Health
See your GP or travel clinic at least 6 weeks before departure for general advice on travel risks and vaccinations. Try phoning a specialist travel clinic if your own doctor is unfamiliar with health conditions in Lebanon. Make sure you have sufficient medical travel insurance, get a dental check, know your own blood group and if you suffer a long-term condition such as diabetes or epilepsy, obtain a Medic Alert bracelet/necklace (www.medicalert.co.uk). If you wear glasses, take a copy of your prescription.

On the whole, standards of hygiene are good, and the health risks are generally very low. As a rule, the worst you can expect is an upset stomach, though more serious food poisoning or gastric infections are not unknown.

The standards of private medical facilities are high in Lebanon. There are plenty of international-standard hospitals in Beirut and even the smaller medical clinics are usually excellent. Note that good medical insurance is absolutely vital.

Vaccinations
Vaccinations are not absolutely necessary, but all the same you are advised to make sure that you are up to date with your **polio**, **diphtheria**, **tetanus**, **typhoid**, **hepatitis A** and **hepatitis B** shots. You may be asked for a **yellow fever** certificate if you have been travelling in a country affected by the disease immediately before travelling to Lebanon. Malaria is not a problem.

Health risks
Tap water is best avoided unless boiled or treated first, so stick to bottled water if you want to be safe. Ice generally gets delivered in a pretty unhygienic fashion, so is best avoided. Raw fruit and vegetables are a potential hazard unless you have washed or peeled them yourself. On the other hand, salads are an integral part of Middle Eastern cuisine and avoiding eating them in some form or other is not entirely practical.

Stomach upsets are common. They're mainly caused by the change in diet (Middle Eastern food is heavy on oil, which can be hard to digest for people unused to this diet). The most common cause of travellers' **diarrhoea** is from eating contaminated food or drinking tap water. Diarrhoea may be also caused by viruses, bacteria (such as E-coli), protozoal (such as giardia), salmonella and cholera. It may be accompanied by vomiting or by severe abdominal pain.

The linchpins of treatment for diarrhoea are rest, fluid and salt replacement, antibiotics such as Ciprofloxacin for the bacterial types and special diagnostic tests and medical treatment for the amoeba and giardia infections. Salmonella infections and cholera, although rare, can be devastating diseases and it would be wise to get to a hospital as soon as possible if these were suspected.

In the summer months **heat exhaustion** and **heatstroke** are common health risks. This is prevented by drinking enough fluids throughout the day (your urine will be pale if you are drinking enough). Symptoms of heat exhaustion and heatstroke are similar and include dizziness, tiredness and headache. Use rehydration salts mixed with water to replenish fluids and salts and find somewhere cool and shady to recover.

If you suspect heatstroke rather than heat exhaustion, you need to cool the body down quickly (cold showers are particularly effective) and may require hospital treatment for electrolyte replacement by intravenous drip.

If you get sick

Contact your embassy or consulate for a list of doctors and dentists who speak your language, or at least some English. Good-quality private healthcare is available in the larger centres but these are expensive; especially hospitalization. Make sure you have adequate insurance (see below).

Useful websites

www.btha.org, British Travel Health Association.
www.fco.gov.uk, British Foreign and Commonwealth Office travel site has useful information on each country, people, climate and a list of UK embassies/consulates.
www.fitfortravel.scot.nhs.uk, A-Z of vaccine/health advice for each country.
www.who.int, World Health Organization site with vaccine and health advice.

Insurance

Take out comprehensive insurance before travel, including full medical cover and extra cover for any activities that you may undertake. Keep details of your policy and the insurance company's telephone number with you at all times and get a police report for any lost or stolen items.

Internet

You'll find internet cafés nearly everywhere across the country with even the smaller towns having at least one internet café, though some can be noisy affairs with half the terminals given over to kids playing video games. The average cost of 1 hour's internet access is 3000 LBP. Wi-Fi is also extremely common, with many hotels offering Wi-Fi access for guests, though most will charge. Many cafés and restaurants in Beirut as well as in other towns and cities offer free Wi-Fi access for customers. Be aware that internet access at many of these free Wi-Fi points can be extremely slow.

Language

Arabic is the national language of Lebanon but the great premium placed on education in the country is reflected in the high levels of fluency in both English and French, even in remote, rural areas. Due to its colonial history **French** remains the most widely spoken language after Arabic. However, amongst the younger generations, **English** is increasingly seen as the more desirable second language.

Media

Lebanon has a thriving media industry which, refreshingly, is the least-censored in the Arab world. Reporting isn't particularly objective though as, despite the fact that the only media restrictions are a ban on defaming the President or other heads of state and on inciting sectarian fighting, much of the media is owned by the separate political/religious factions and so operate to their own agenda.

The *Daily Star* is the English-language daily newspaper, while a weekly magazine, *Monday Morning*, wraps up the previous week's headlines and includes interesting features on national and regional issues alongside plenty of features on Lebanon's high society social scene. The French-language daily is *L'Orient le Jour*, which is a condensed version of the Arabic-language daily *An Nahar*. It includes useful listings of events in Lebanon. There are in addition numerous Arabic-language papers, some of them independent, others propaganda organs for various political parties and religious groups. All the major foreign newspapers and magazines are readily available in Beirut, though they are expensive.

Radio Liban, which is controlled by the Ministry of Information, broadcasts on 96.2 MHz (FM). It has daily French-language broadcasts at 1800. There are numerous other radio stations within Lebanon, many of which can only be picked up over a relatively small area. Explore the radio waves for yourself. On the whole they broadcast a diet of either Arabic or Western pop music (or sometimes a mixture of the 2), along with various chat shows and phone-ins. **Radio One** broadcasts on 105.5 MHz (FM) and can be picked up over most of the country. It is styled on the BBC's Radio 1 in the UK and often has visiting DJs from there. The best frequency for receiving the **BBC World Service** is 1323 kHz (MW), although it is also available on 720 kHz (MW) and in various SW bands. **Voice of America** is on 1260 kHz (AM).

There are numerous **television** stations in Lebanon, nearly all of which represent a political or religious faction. **Télé Liban** is the only government-controlled TV station. It broadcasts on 3 channels and has programmes in Arabic, French and English. Of the private TV stations, the 2 most popular are; the **Lebanese Broadcasting Company (LBC)**, established in 1985 by the 'Lebanese Forces' Christian militia of Samir Geagea; and **Future TV**, set up by the late Prime Minister, Rafiq Hariri. Both now have broad popular appeal and show plenty of foreign programmes. The controversial TV station **Al-Manar** is sponsored by Hezbollah. Most hotels have satellite TV, and generally subscribe to all the major international channels.

On the **internet**, the English-language daily news site www.yaliban.com is a leading advocate of free, completely uncensored media and is an excellent source of information.

Money
→ €1 = 2166 LBP, £1 = 2463 LBP, US$1 = 1512 LBP (May 2011)

The basic unit of currency is the **Lebanese pound (LBP)**, also referred to as the Lebanese Lira (LL). Notes come in denominations of 1000, 5000, 10,000, 20,000, 50,000 and 100,000. Coins come in denominations of 250 and 500. In addition, the US$ operates as a parallel currency, interchangeable with the LBP, and most transactions (for example in shops, restaurants, bars and hotels) can be made in dollars rather than LBP or in a mixture of the two. Be aware that even if you pay for your transaction in dollars you will usually only get your change back in LBP.

Changing or accessing money is generally very easy, though one exception to this is changing travellers' cheques, which can be surprisingly difficult.

ATMs
Except in very rural areas, you should have no problem finding an ATM. Many ATMs allow you to choose to take your money out in either LBP or US$. In general Visa is the most widely accepted card.

Cash
Major currencies (UK£, US$ and €) can be exchanged at banks and at all money changers; the latter will charge you a commission fee, so shop around. The US$ is the most convenient currency and can be used in day-to-day transactions. Notes in smaller denominations are easier to exchange.

It is always useful to have some hard currency with you, for the odd occasion when all the ATMs in town decide not to hand out any cash (rare but not unheard of), and for using for visas, etc when crossing borders. Be aware that, although leftover

Syrian currency can be exchanged at most banks in Beirut, the same cannot be said for Lebanese currency in Syria. Be sure to exchange any leftover LBP at the border.

Credit cards

All the major credit cards are recognized. As well as being accepted in most hotels, restaurants and shops, nearly all the banks in Lebanon will allow you to draw money against major credit (or debit) cards and also have ATMs that can be used in the same way.

Transferring money

Western Union Money Transfer, (www.westernunion.com) is represented in Lebanon by Byblos Bank and the Lebanese-Canadian Bank (amongst others). The fees charged are very high, but this can be a good emergency option.

Traveller's cheques (TCs)

If you are intending to carry your money in this form, make sure that you have US$ TCs, as TCs in any other currency are extremely hard to exchange. All banks charge a commission for changing TCs; though the fee is usually only around 1%, they all apply a minimum charge of US$5, and in some cases an additional US$2 'handling' fee. You will also be asked to produce the original purchase slip (even though this is supposed to be kept separate from the TCs). Most money changers charge around 4-5% commission for changing US$ TCs, and are extremely reluctant to deal with TCs in any other currency.

Cost of living and travelling

The cost of living and travelling is more expensive than in neighbouring Syria, mostly due to the cost of accommodation and eating. The vast majority of hotels fall into the mid-range and luxury categories (from around US$50 for a double room upwards), with the luxury end of the market being heavily over-represented. That said,

there are a limited number of cheaper hotels to be found, as well as a few genuine budget places where you can get a bed in a dormitory for as low as US$10.

Eating out is also comparatively expensive, though is still good value compared to Europe; a meal in a restaurant will generally cost a minimum of US$10 per head, and around US$15 will be closer to the norm, while in the more expensive restaurants, the sky's the limit. To eat cheaply, you have to restrict yourself to a diet of takeaway food and give Lebanon's extensive restaurant scene a miss.

Likewise, if you plan to indulge in Lebanon's vibrant nightlife, be prepared to shell out as much for the evening as you would in Europe, North America or Australasia. In contrast, buying alcohol from a shop (both wine and beer) is actually reasonably priced.

Public transport is cheap, with the furthest journeys costing around 6000 LBP, and most ranging in price from 2000-4000 LBP. Entrance tickets are fairly priced with most sites costing between 5000-12,000 LBP.

Sticking to the very strictest of budgets, it is possible to survive in Lebanon on around US$25 per day as long as you use dormitory accommodation, eat off the street vendors and limit your sightseeing. It's more realistic to budget for at least US$30 per day and know that as soon as you start to treat yourself a little, this will quickly rise. A mid-range budget (a/c hotels, restaurant meals and perhaps a hire car) involves a big step up to around US$80 per day. At the luxury end of the scale, you are looking at a minimum of around US$200 per day.

Opening hours

Banks: Mon-Fri 0800-1400 and Sat 0830-1200. Government offices and post offices: Mon-Sat 0800-1400. Shops: Mon-Fri 0900-2000 and Sat 0900-1500, though some will keep shorter or longer hours on Sat and some open on Sun as well. Money Exchange Offices in Beirut and other major towns usually stay open for longer hours than the banks. **Major sights**: generally Tue-Sun from 0900-1800 in summer and 0900-1600 in winter, though some sights open 7 days a week.

Post
Postal services are run by the private **Liban Post** (www.libanpost.com.lb), whose distinctive blue and yellow logo is prominently displayed outside post offices in all towns and cities. **Postcards** to Europe cost 1000 LBP and take 2-4 days to arrive, while to North America, Australia and New Zealand they cost 1500 LBP and usually take 1 week. **Letters** (up to 20 g) to all these regions cost 1750 LBP.

You can send **parcels** weighing up to 10 kg through the Lebanese postal system. A parcel weighing 1 kg to Europe, North America, Australia or New Zealand costs 31,500 LBP while a 2 kg parcel costs 58,000 LBP. If you want a faster delivery and the security of parcel tracking you can use Liban Post's more expensive **international express delivery** service. With this service a 1 kg parcel to Europe costs 56,000 LBP; to North America, 60,000 LBP; and to Australia and New Zealand, 80,000 LBP.

All post offices in Lebanon provide **poste restante** services. Mail must be addressed in the following way: your name, Liban Post, the post office's name, poste restante, Lebanon. Mail will be held for you for 2 months. When collecting mail, you will need to bring your passport as proof of identification.

Prohibitions
Drugs
Possession of narcotics is illegal. Those caught in possession risk a long prison sentence and/or deportation. There is a marked intolerance to drug taking in the country and the drugs scene is distinctly seedy (not to mention paranoid) and is best avoided.

Photography
Avoid taking pictures of military installations or anything that might be construed as 'sensitive', particularly if you are close to the Israeli border.

Safety
Having been emblazoned on everyone's mind as a place of brutal and interminable civil war, suicide bombings and hostage taking, Lebanon is still, years later, trying to shake off its negative media image. In recent years the country has suffered from sporadic outbreaks of violence, the 2006 July War being one period when Lebanon was yet again thrust under the media spotlight for all the wrong reasons. For the past 2 years Lebanon has been undergoing an essentially stable period that has brought tourists flooding back. Although sporadic outbreaks of violence do occur, if you use good judgment, today's Lebanon is essentially a perfectly safe place in which to travel.

Ordinary crime and the threat of personal violence are minimal compared to Europe and North America, though more of a problem than in other Arab countries. Provided you take the usual precautions (never leave valuables unattended in hotel rooms, use hotel safes where available and when hotel safes are not available keep your money and important documents out of sight, on your person, preferably in a money belt or something similar), you should have no problem. Note that petty crime such as bag snatching is on the rise in the main cities, though occurrences are minimal compared to in the West.

Many foreign office travel advisory sites still warn that none but essential travel should be undertaken to the south of the country and to certain areas in the Bekaa Valley due to several occasions in recent years when the security situation has rapidly deteriorated with little warning. Although it is, of course, extremely important to keep yourself up to date with events before travelling here, normally these days travel in these areas is safe. The area south of the Litani River is under UNIFIL control and certain travel restrictions, which change frequently, do apply for foreigners.

If you want to visit one of the Palestinian refugee camps, it's best to do so with a well-informed local escort. Shatila is probably the easiest to visit and the Shatila Camp Children and Youth Centre (www.cycshatila. org) run a guesthouse within the camp for visitors.

If you'd like to visit the south be aware that unexploded ordnance is still a problem in the area south of the Litani River, despite a massive demining operation. If you are in this area it is essential that you stick to the roads and avoid walking in open countryside.

The most recent cross-border attack in the south occurred in Aug 2010 when an Israeli military tree-uprooting operation caused a full-out gun battle between Lebanese Army and Israeli Defence Force troops, leaving 4 people dead. There is always the risk of fresh outbreaks of violence. Ultimately, it is really a question of using your common sense and weighing up the risks for yourself. Bear in mind that even when there has been a flare-up of fighting in the far south, the rest of the country is still perfectly safe to visit.

The biggest danger tourists face while in the country is on the roads. Lebanese driving is erratic at best and absolutely petrifying at the worst (see page 10).

Student travellers
Anyone in full-time education is entitled to an **International Student Identity Card** (ISIC). These are issued by student travel offices and travel agencies across the world. In Lebanon, an ISIC card entitles you to a discount entry fee at some of the major sites (including the National Museum in Beirut, Baalbek and Tyre's El Mina and El Bass ruins).

Tax
Airport departure tax
The airport departure tax of US$42 is levied on all flights from Rafiq Hariri International Airport and is usually included in the cost of your ticket, but be sure to check that this is the case.

Other taxes
There is no land departure tax when leaving from Lebanon.

Most top-end hotels and restaurants charge an extra 10% tax on top of your total, some also add a further service charge.

Telephone
To call Lebanon from overseas dial your international access code, followed by Lebanon's country code **961** and then the area/town code. To call an international phone number from within Lebanon dial **00**, followed by the country code.

To call Syria from Lebanon you dial **02** followed by the city code (dropping the initial zero). For example: to call Damascus from Lebanon, dial 0211 followed by the number.

Most travellers are able to use their mobile phones in Lebanon – ask your provider before you travel. Using a phone overseas can be expensive, so don't forget to check your provider's roaming rates.

Lebanon has 2 mobile phone networks: **Alfa** and **MTC**. If you have an unlocked phone you can purchase a local SIM card to use while in Lebanon. Pay-as-you-go SIM cards in Lebanon are quite pricey so it's probably not worth doing unless you are going to spend a decent amount of time in the country. Any of the multitude phone shops in Beirut and other large centres can get you started.

The cheapest way to make local and international calls is by using the extensive network of card-operated public telephones. The cards to use in these phones (**Telecartes**) can be purchased at most grocery stores. A card with 10,000 LBP phone credit costs 11,000 LBP.

Time

2 hrs ahead of GMT Oct-Mar, and 3 hrs ahead Apr-Sep.

Tipping

Lebanon has a more relaxed attitude to tipping than other neighbouring countries. In general it is standard to leave a small tip for anyone who helps you (hotel porters, etc) and it's also normal practice to round up your private taxi fare so that the driver receives a small tip. The standard 10% is acceptable in more expensive restaurants; otherwise it is really down to your own discretion. Remember that the more expensive restaurants often add a service charge onto their bill.

Tour operators

Cyclamen, T03-486551, www.tlb-destinations.com. This responsible travel operator and hiking club runs trips throughout Lebanon with 1-day hikes and activity trips scheduled for most Sun throughout the year as well as longer small-group trips and tours. The weekly day trips range from snowshoeing in the Chouf Mountains to hiking in the Bekaa, and usually cost 35,000 LBP. Group tours all have a focus on promoting rural tourism or use small family-run guesthouses and homestays. Proceeds made from running the trips go towards tourism training in rural areas.

Esprit Nomade, T03-223552, www.esprit-nomade.com. This is another company who operates weekly activity and hiking trips which anyone can join, as well as having a range of private trips that travellers can book. The weekly day trips cover a whole range of activities such as sea kayaking, rafting, hiking and caving.

Liban Trek, T01-329975, www.libantrek.com. Lebanon's first ecotourism tour company specializes in putting together private tour itineraries that focus on culture, nature, adventure sports or a combination of the 3. They also run day trips that anyone can join, with departures throughout the year, usually costing 35,000 LBP including return transport and local guides. The day trips are generally trekking-based, commonly using one of Lebanon's national reserves or going along one of the Lebanon Mountain Trail routes.

Responsible Mobilities, T03-218048, www.responsible.mobilities.com. Run by Pascal Abdullah, who was previously the force behind Cyclamen and has been heavily involved in responsible tourism initiatives in Lebanon for years. Responsible Mobilities can set up private tour itineraries of any length all over the country. They are focused on sustainable development and conserving the environment. Tours give travellers a rare glimpse into Lebanese rural life, and often involve seasonal agricultural work such as fruit picking and staying in homestays.

Vamos Todos, T03-561174, www.vamos-todos.com. This hiking club runs day trips every Sun. Trips range from hiking in the Qadisha Valley to visiting the Palm Island Reserve off Tripoli's coast. They also run longer weekend trips that involve caving, rafting and all sorts of other adventure sports.

Tourist information

The Lebanon Tourism Board has offices abroad in France and Egypt. They also operate an excellent website (see below) packed full of useful information on Lebanon for travellers. Once in Lebanon, the main tourist information office is located in the centre of West Beirut and is well stocked with pamphlets and maps. There is also a branch at Rafiq Hariri International Airport and smaller branches in Tripoli, Sidon, Zahle and Byblos.

Useful websites

www.lebanon-tourism.gov.lb, the Ministry of Tourism's official website for Lebanon.
www.lebanontourism.org, useful site full of practical information for visitors.
www.lebanontourist.com, informative and helpful site covering the country.

www.tourism-lebanon.com, packed full of information on Lebanon's sights and attractions.

www.fco.gov.uk, homepage of the British Foreign and Commonwealth Office; gives current safety recommendations regarding travel in Lebanon.

Visas and immigration

A passport valid for at least 6 months beyond your intended period of stay is required to enter Lebanon.

Nationals of the following countries are able to obtain a **free single-entry 1-month tourist visa** (which is extendable up to a 3-month period) on arrival at any official point of entry into Lebanon: Andorra, Antigua and Barbuda, Argentina, Armenia, Australia, Austria, Azerbaijan, The Bahamas, Barbados, Belarus, Belgium, Belize, Bhutan, Brazil, Bulgaria, Canada, Chile, China, Czech Republic, Costa Rica, Croatia, Cyprus, Denmark, Dominican Republic, Estonia, Finland, France, Great Britain, Georgia, Germany, Greece, Hong Kong, Hungary, Iceland, Ireland, Italy, Japan, Kazakhstan, Kyrgyzstan, Latvia, Lithuania, Liechtenstein, Luxembourg, Macedonia, Macau, Malaysia, Malta, Mexico, Moldova, Monaco, Montenegro, Netherlands, New Zealand, Norway, Palau, Panama, Peru, Poland, Portugal, Russia, Romania, Saint Kitts and Nevis, Samoa, San Marina, Serbia, Singapore, Slovakia, Slovenia, South Korea, Spain, Sweden, Switzerland, Tajikistan, Turkey (only at the airport), Turkmenistan, USA, Ukraine, Uzbekistan, Venezuela and Yugoslavia. Nationals of all other countries have to apply for a visa before they arrive (50,000 LBP) from the Lebanese Embassy in their home country.

Visa requirements to Lebanon do change sporadically. For up-to-date information see the website of the Lebanese General Security Office, www.general-security.gov.lb.

Note You will not be issued with a visa or allowed entry into Lebanon, even with a visa, if there is any evidence of a visit to Israel in your passport.

Extending your visa

Once in Lebanon, 1-month tourist visas can be extended up to a total period of 3 months at the **Lebanese General Security Office** in Beirut. To apply for an extension wait until the last few days of your visa and then head to the office with your passport, 2 photocopies of your passport ID and visa pages and 2 passport photos (see page 78).

Weights and measures
Metric.

Women travellers

Lebanon is arguably the most liberal of all the Middle Eastern countries and on the surface there doesn't seem to be any difference in attitudes to those in Europe or North America. Lebanese women are highly fashionable and the glossy magazine image of the ideal Lebanese woman is one who divides her time between fitness/body toning activities, hair and beauty treatments, designer shopping and a high-society world of wining and dining. In reality, however, for the majority of the population, the unspoken rules governing relationships and sexual behaviour remain more conservative (amongst both Christians and Muslims) than initial impressions may lead you to believe. The majority of women live with their families until they are married and most are carefully chaperoned and protected from any possibility of bringing 'dishonour' to the family.

Travelling as a solo foreign woman in Lebanon is in general problem-free and you probably won't encounter any issues. Although you may attract some attention from Lebanese males, on the whole it tends to be good natured and polite. The most common annoyance for solo female travellers is simply the constant questioning of why you aren't married. If you do experience any come-ons that are threatening or unpleasant, make your feelings known clearly and firmly. Like everywhere else in the Middle East this sort of behaviour is considered shameful and not to be tolerated, and you'll find people will run to your aid. Some female travellers have reported experiencing harassment while using public transport, particularly while using service taxis in Beirut. If possible always take the back seat of a service taxi. If at any stage you feel uncomfortable, tell the driver to stop the car and get out.

However liberal attitudes may appear to be towards women's dress in cosmopolitan areas, as soon as you head into more traditional areas attitudes are much more conservative. You will garner much more respect if you wear modest clothing.

Working and volunteering

Most people who come to work in Lebanon come with a job already organized. Qualified teachers (of all subjects) can quite easily find jobs with the international schools in Beirut (who teach in English), although these usually only hire once a year. There also may be opportunities for writers and copy-editors with the many English and French-language publications.

There are huge opportunities for volunteering, mostly with organizations involved with helping the Palestine refugees. 2 excellent associations are the **Insan Association** (www.insanassociation. org) and the **Shatila Camp Children and Youth Centre (CYC)** (www.cycshatila.org). Both the British organization **UNIPAL** (www. unipal.org.uk) and the Canadian **CEPAL** (www.cepal.ca) arrange volunteer English-teaching positions. **Kafa** (www.kafa.org.lb) is an NGO targeting violence against women inside the country, while **Right to Play** (www.righttoplay.com) is focused on letting disadvantaged kids play sports.

Contents

Footprint features

Beirut

Ins and outs

Airport information

Rafiq Hariri International Airport, 10 km to the south of the city centre, is the only airport in Lebanon and handles all the international flights into and out of the country. There are ATMs, money exchange, at least six car rental firms and a couple of restaurants in the arrivals hall. A fast dual carriageway runs between the centre of town and the airport and, depending on traffic, a journey into central Beirut takes around 30 minutes. The easiest way to get into town is by taxi, and you'll have no trouble finding one in front of the terminal. The fare price varies enormously, depending on your bargaining skills and the time of day or night. You can expect offers to start at around a hilariously exorbitant US$40, though they will rapidly fall to around US$20 with a bit of bargaining. Walking determinedly out of the arrivals lounge into the parking area invariably gets things moving a bit more quickly. Skilled bargainers should be able to get the price down to US$10-15. At night, or in the early hours of the morning, it is considerably harder to get prices down.

Unfortunately catching a bus from the airport entails a bit of a hike. You must walk for just over 1 km to the roundabout at the entrance to the airport complex. From here you can catch LCC bus No 5 all the way to Ain el-Mreisse (on the Corniche opposite McDonalds), going via Cola Junction bus station, Raouche and along the seafront. However, these buses only run roughly 0630-1730 and the journey takes around one hour. There are also minibuses and service taxis that run between the roundabout outside the airport complex and the road junction known as Balbirs (near the Hippodrome, from where there are buses and service taxis into the centre), but again, these only run during the day. ▶▶ *See Transport, page 49.*

Getting around

Beirut isn't the easiest city to get around, to say the least. New arrivals are usually confused by the spaghetti sprawl of different districts and the rocket-pace of the traffic, which makes crossing the road an adventure in itself. Unfortunately the public transport system – provided by a mix of service taxis, public and private buses and microbuses – doesn't help, and even a lot of the locals seem to be stumped by the seemingly mysterious routes of some of the buses. A list of some of the more handy bus routes is given on page 50.

The easiest (and most popular) form of public transport are the spluttering **service taxis**. These shared taxis buzz around the roads of the city constantly picking up passengers. All you have to do is wait by the side of the road and wave one down. When the driver slows down, shout the name of your destination and he'll either stop for you to get in or speed away. If the first one doesn't want to take you there'll soon be another car trundling along.

If you're going somewhere the driver wasn't intending to go he may want to take you as a private taxi passenger, which will mean you'll be the only passenger and you'll be taken directly to your destination. In a service taxi, the driver will pick up and drop off passengers along the way so you'll probably take a more roundabout route. Obviously in a service taxi you pay a lot less for your fare, so if you don't want to pay a private taxi passenger fare make sure you say '*serveece*' to the driver when you get in. See page 51 for more information on service taxis.

There are also various companies that operate **private taxis** inside the city. These are usually distinguishable by their colour (usually yellow or white) and the company insignia along the car's body. They usually have air conditioning and are in a much better condition than the older service taxis. You can hail them off the street or you can phone them to book a pickup.

Walking Beirut

In a city renowned for being pedestrian-unfriendly, a walking tour may seem like a strange idea. However, Ronnie Chatah, the brains behind Walk Beirut's city tour, has created an itinerary that not only works but also gives travellers an insightful and fascinating introduction to Lebanon's capital.

Over a four-hour period, and using as many back roads and side streets as possible, you'll meander from Hamra, through central Beirut and onto Monot. Along the way Ronnie Chatah (who still guides most of the walks himself) weaves the story of this city's past, giving you an insider's look into the ever-changing face of this capital. Grand, old, neo-Ottoman buildings now falling into a state of sad disrepair; the now defunct cinema on Rue Hamra where Palestinian guerrillas would watch action-flicks in between bouts of fighting; Downtown's excavated Roman bath complex and the bullet-pocked statue of Martyr's Square: Beirut's complex and compelling history is put into context by the legends and tales behind its buildings.

For any new arrival to the capital, Walk Beirut's city tour is a must-do if you're interested in delving deeper into this city's multitude layers of history. See page 48 for tour booking information.

Although it may seem daunting at first, Beirut can actually be a great city for walking. The trick is to catch a taxi or service taxi for the journeys between the districts and then set off on foot to explore. In particular, the districts of Hamra, Ras Beirut and Gemmayze are funky and happening places to wander around. Those interested in discovering Beirut on foot should take note of the city tour offered by **Walk Beirut**, which provides an excellent introduction to the city, see box, above.

Orientation

Beirut forms a headland bounded to the north and west by the Mediterranean and to the east by the southernmost reaches of Mount Lebanon. Today the Green Line that divided Beirut (marked by Rue de Damas) is still distinguishable by the concentration of bullet-pocked and bombed-out buildings that lie along it, and while it no longer exists as a physical barrier, the division of the city between Christian east and Muslim west is as marked as ever.

West Beirut is focused on Hamra, which following the destruction of the old Downtown area became the business and commercial centre of the city with most of the hotels, restaurants, banks, shops and other services. To the north of Hamra are the grounds of the American University of Beirut (AUB), while to the west are the exclusive districts of Ras Beirut and Manara overlooking the western Mediterranean seaboard. Ain el-Mreisse forms a small area to the northeast of Hamra, while extending to the east of it is the new Downtown area, now known as the Beirut Central District. At its eastern edge is Beirut's port complex. Extending south from the port up the hill are the Christian areas of East Beirut, a series of districts climbing up to Achrafieh, the most elegant of them. Sprawling south towards the airport are the poverty-stricken and ramshackle southern suburbs (known collectively as the *dahiya*), home to the city's Shiite population and the Palestinian refugee camps.

Tourist information

Tourist information office ⓘ *ground floor of the Ministry of Tourism building, corner of Rue Banque du Liban/Rue de Rome, T01-340940, www.destinationlebanon.gov.lb, summer Mon-*

Sat 0800-1800, winter 0800-1600. You have to walk through the ground floor car park to get to the office. They have a good selection of pamphlets on all the main tourist attractions in Lebanon, as well as a decent free map of Beirut. The staff are generally friendly and helpful, although their usefulness in terms of practical information and advice is somewhat limited. The **tourist police** are based in the same building.

Background

Pre and early history Various stone implements discovered in the vicinity of Beirut reveal evidence of human activity dating back as far as the **Palaeolithic** era, although exactly when a permanent settlement was first established here is not known. Excavations in the redevelopment area of central Beirut have revealed traces of a **Canaanite** settlement, the earliest phases of which appear to go back to the 19th-18th century BC.

In the **Phoenician** period after around 1200 BC, despite its favourable location close to reliable water sources and with a sheltered natural harbour, Beirut was largely eclipsed by the more important Phoenician cities of Sidon, Tyre and Byblos. Certainly, the historical record is all but silent as to its fate, while the other coastal cities find frequent mention in Assyrian, Babylonian and Persian records. Although not mentioned in accounts of Alexander the Great's conquest of the coastal cities, Beirut does reappear in later **Hellenistic** records, named *Laodicea in Canaan*, possibly by the Seleucid emperor Antiochus IV in the second century BC (a total of five cities were named *Laodicea* by the Seleucids in honour of a Seleucid queen, *Laodice*). Excavations carried out in 1994 have confirmed that the later Roman city closely followed a typical grid pattern of streets that was essentially of Hellenistic origin.

Roman Period The city only really began to flourish during the **Roman** period, becoming an important commercial port and military base. It was first conquered by the emperor Pompey in 64 BC. Later, the emperor Augustus (r 27 BC to AD 14, formerly Octavian) placed it under the governorship of Vespasianus Agrippa, the husband of his daughter Julia, raising it to the status of a colony and renaming it *Colonia Julia Augusta Felix Berytus* in her honour.

An extensive city was laid out over the earlier Hellenistic foundations, and baths, markets, a theatre and other public buildings erected. The Herodian kings of Judaea (which was at that time in effect a Roman client-state) financed many of these building works in order to gain favour with the Romans. Veterans from the V Macedonica and VIII Gallica legions were given land and settled there, while the local inhabitants received Roman citizenship and were exempted from taxes. From AD 190-200 the Roman emperor Septimus Severus established a School of Law at Beirut, and from the early third century the city flourished as one of the great centres of Roman jurisprudence. It was here that the substance of the famous Code of Justinian, to which the Western legal system owes its origins, was developed by Papiniam and Ulpian. Beirut was unique in that culturally it was distinctively Roman, with its Law School and community of veterans, in contrast to other cities where Hellenistic cultural influences remained strongest.

Byzantines, catastrophe and Crusader control Beirut continued to flourish during the **Byzantine** period, not least because of the fame of its Law School, becoming the seat of a bishopric by the end of the fourth century. Its reputation as a commercial centre was enhanced meanwhile by the manufacture and trade in silk. However, in AD 551 the city was all but destroyed by earthquakes and associated tidal waves. The Law School was moved to Sidon and although Beirut was subsequently rebuilt, it never regained its former glory. When it fell to the Muslim Arab conquest in AD 635, it was still a relatively insignificant port, and remained so for nearly four centuries of Arab rule.

In 1110 it was captured by Baldwin I after a lengthy siege, and remained in **Crusader** hands until 1187 when it was retaken by Salah ud-Din. Just six years later, however, it was occupied by Amoury, king of Cyprus, so passing back into Crusader hands. In 1291 it was captured by the **Mamluks** and the Crusaders were driven out for the last time. There were a number of attempts to recapture it during the 14th century, but ultimately when Europeans started to settle there during the 15th century, they came as traders rather than conquerors.

Ottomans and oligarchs In 1516 the Mamluks were defeated by Sultan Selim I and Beirut subsequently became part of the **Ottoman Empire**. However, Ottoman rule was never directly applied, local rulers being appointed instead and given a large degree of autonomy provided they faithfully collected and passed on the taxes that were due. Two local rulers were particularly notable for their role in reviving Beirut's commercial reputation. **Emir Fakhr ud-Din II Maan** (1590-1635) was perhaps the most powerful and famous of Lebanon's local rulers during the Ottoman period. During the 18th century Beirut's fortunes fluctuated, favoured for a while by one Emir, only to be neglected by the next. It began to flourish more consistently under **Emir Bashir Shihab II** (1788-1840). However, he also laid the seeds of his own downfall in 1832 by entering into an alliance with **Ibrahim Pasha**, the son of the viceroy of Egypt Mohammad Ali, who had risen against the Ottoman Empire and was threatening to overthrow it. Britain was alarmed at this upset to the balance of power in the region and the threat it posed to her interests. In 1840 a combined Anglo-Austro-Turkish fleet bombarded Beirut. Emir Bashir was captured and sent into exile and direct Ottoman rule was re-established. The opening up of Damascus to European trade from this time fuelled ever greater commercial activity in Beirut, along with an increasing European presence.

In 1860, the massacre of Maronites at the hands of the Druze, first in Lebanon and then in Damascus, prompted direct European military intervention. French troops landed in Beirut and thousands of Maronites fled to the city for protection. These events led to the establishment of 'Mount Lebanon' as a semi-autonomous province, although Beirut itself remained under direct Ottoman control. With its population vastly expanded by the influx of Maronites, and with an ever growing European presence, Beirut's position as the commercial capital of the eastern Mediterranean was further enhanced.

The French Mandate and early years as Lebanon's capital During the **First World War** the British, French and Russian navies blockaded Beirut's port in an attempt to dislodge the Ottoman military forces from Lebanon. This, combined with a series of natural disasters, brought famine to the country on a massive scale. In 1916 the leaders of a local revolt against the Ottomans were executed in Beirut, in what afterwards became known as Martyrs' Square. On the 8 October 1918, eight days after the fall of Damascus, the British army entered Beirut with a detachment of French troops. Under the provisions of the secretly negotiated **Sykes-Picot treaty** of 1916, Lebanon (as part of Syria) was placed under **French Mandate** rule in April 1920. Under pressure from the Maronites, the French promptly created the new, enlarged state of 'Grand Liban' (Greater Lebanon), separate from Syria and with Beirut as its capital. The inter-war years were peaceful ones in which Beirut was able to consolidate its position as capital of the new state.

The Second World War and the Arab-Israeli war The **Second World War** saw the return of Allied troops to Beirut, with full independence only being established for the country in

Visiting the camps

There are Palestinian refugee camps on the outskirts of Beirut, Tyre and Tripoli but the easiest ones to visit are Sabra and Shatila in Beirut's southern suburbs.

In Shatila there is no such thing as privacy. The concrete block buildings loom claustrophobically close from the narrow alleys between. There is only sporadic electricity and the residents have no access to running drinking water. There isn't a hint of greenery here; even the school doesn't have a playground. Yet the resilient inhabitants of Shatila have learnt to adapt and survive in this depressing environment.

Although the camps should never be treated as a tourist attraction, those travellers genuinely interested in the plight of the Palestinians will find a warm welcome. Despite what you may hear, Shatila and Sabra are both open and easily accessible, though it makes sense to keep up to date with current events before considering a visit here. The CYC is an excellent contact in Shatila and are happy to help any foreign visitors inside the camp. Travellers should note to dress conservatively before a visit (clothes covering the body down to the ankles and wrists) and to be especially sensitive about taking photos.

1946. Since independence the fate of Beirut has always been closely linked to, and shaped by, the country's (and indeed the wider region's) complex and tumultuous history.

The **Arab-Israeli war** of 1947-1949 resulted in a massive influx of Palestine refugees, most of whom were settled in camps in the southern part of the city and remain there until the present day (see page 26). When tensions over support for Nasser's pan-Arab vision degenerated into civil war in 1958, some 15,000 US Marines landed in Beirut to restore order. In 1970 the PLO, having been driven out of Jordan, set up their headquarters in Beirut, launching frequent attacks on Israel and establishing themselves as a virtual 'state within a state'.

Civil War When all-out **civil war** finally erupted in 1975, Beirut was the main focus for the fighting. The city became divided by the infamous **Green Line** between Muslim West Beirut and Christian East Beirut. The devastation and suffering was on an unprecedented scale and continued more or less unabated through Syrian occupation, Israeli invasion and the presence of various United Nations and multinational peace-keeping forces. Worst hit was the Downtown area, which was literally flattened after 15 years of war. Fighting eventually subsided in 1989 and by 1991 the Green Line had been dismantled, finally heralding a lasting peace.

Modern Beirut Beirut's reconstruction after the war was very much the vision of Rafiq Hariri, prime minister of the country for much of the 1990s. His vastly ambitious plan for the city's new Downtown area, and the massive spiralling debt that his construction plans burdened Lebanon with, have been a highly controversial issue in the post-civil war years.

Beirut enjoyed a period of relative stability from the end of the civil war up to 2005, but the city's calm unravelled on **14 February 2005** when a massive bomb blast detonated outside the St George Hotel on the Corniche tearing apart the passing motorcade of ex-prime minister Rafiq Hariri resulting in his death along with 22 others. The days after the bombing saw Beirut's Downtown area submerged under a sea of rival demonstration rallies with Martyr's Square the focus for the protesters. Out of these massive demonstrations came the birth of the

'**Cedar Revolution**', which resulted in the eventual withdrawal of Syrian troops from Lebanon.

During the **July war** of 2006 Beirut suffered heavy damage from Israeli shelling. Although the central city area was left alone the Israeli's targeted much of the city's surrounding infrastructure with the international airport along with many roads and bridges leading into the capital being damaged and destroyed. Israel's main targets in the city though were within the sprawling southern suburbs, known collectively as the *Dahia*. As Hezbollah's urban heartland and home to their headquarters this area suffered major devastation during the month long bombardment. Hundreds of civilians were killed and entire streets were reduced to ruin. Reconstruction in this area (much of it sponsored directly by Hezbollah and by donations from Iran) has, since 2006, been astonishingly fast.

The period from December 2006 to May 2008 saw Downtown Beirut once again become the focus for mass protests. This time it was Hezbollah-led anti-government factions who took over Downtown, and the massive tent-city set up near the Serail caused a 17-month hiatus to normal business taking place in the city's main commercial and financial district. The protest was only dismantled in May 2008 following the election of Michel Sulieman as president of the country and the formation of a national unity government.

Since mid-2008 Beirut has enjoyed a relative period of stability. The city has been able to flourish, though only time will tell if this will be sustained long term. With modern Beirut the embodiment of so many of the hopes and aspirations, as well as the frustrations and fears, of modern Lebanon, the city's survival is very much tied to the wider fate of the country as a whole.

National Museum

① Tue-Sun 0900-1700, 5000 LBP, students 1000 LBP, guided tours 20,000 LBP. An audio visual introduction begins once an hour, on the hour, in a room to the right of the ticket office. The museum shop sells high-quality replicas, souvenirs and postcards.

Opened again to the public in 1999, the National Museum is the jewel in the crown of Beirut's cultural heritage and a powerful symbol of the city's regeneration. It boasts a superb collection of excellently presented artefacts, with everything labelled in English, French and Arabic, while information boards provide brief outlines of each period.

Background Situated right on the Green Line, separating East and West Beirut, the museum took a pounding during the civil war. Some of the artefacts were removed for safekeeping when hostilities broke out, while the larger ones, such as the stone sarcophagi and mosaics that could not easily be removed, were sealed within thick concrete shells in order to protect them from damage. After the war the museum was the focus of a massive restoration project. Not only did the building itself have to be extensively repaired, but the museum's collection had also suffered severe damage, not least because the basement, where many items were stored, became flooded.

The audio visual hall in the museum's entrance lobby shows a short video giving a quick history of the founding of the museum as well as fascinating footage of the building at the end of the war, revealing the full extent of the devastation.

Visiting the museum As you enter, you are first confronted by a large **mosaic** depicting Calliope, the muse of philosophy, surrounded by Socrates and the seven wise men all framed within ornate roundels. Dating from the third century AD, this beautiful mosaic was discovered at Baalbek, in the dining room of a Roman villa. In the central area of the hall, arranged around the mosaic, are four large marble **sarcophagi** discovered at Tyre and dating from the second century AD. The delicately carved reliefs adorning their sides depict scenes of drunken banquets and epic battles from the legend of Achilles, and show a quite remarkable degree of artistry in their execution.

In the hall to your right are various artefacts from the Sanctuary of Eshmoun near Sidon, the most striking of which are the statuettes of young children and babies, offered by parents in thanks for the healing of their children. Dating from the fifth century BC, they already show clear Greek influences, even though Alexander the Great did not arrive in the region until a century later.

In the hall opposite are various artefacts from the first and second millenniums BC, including the **sarcophagus of Ahiram**, king of Byblos (10th century BC). Though rather clumsily carved in comparison with the Roman sarcophagi from Tyre, its significance is enormous in that it is inscribed with the earliest known example of the Phoenician alphabet, upon which our own Latin one is based. Many of the artefacts here are of Egyptian origin, or else Egyptian-inspired, notably the stele of the Pharaoh Ramses II, complete with a hieroglyphic inscription, found at Tyre. Dominating the small room at the far end of this hall is a carved Colossus from Byblos, also Egyptian in style. Equally striking is the reconstruction of a marble column base in the shape of a pumpkin, and a capital decorated with carved bulls' heads, both from the fifth century BC Sidon.

Tucked away in the corner to the left of the stairs leading up to the first floor is a beautiful fragment of Roman mural from Tyre depicting a figure carrying a load on his shoulder, the colours still surprisingly vivid. In the corner to the right of the stairs is a Roman carved limestone altar from Niha in the Bekaa Valley, with two lions flanking a central god. Flanking the stairs themselves are two graceful and beautifully preserved marble statues, the one on the right being Hygeia, goddess of health, while the one on the left is an unidentified Roman woman, clearly of noble blood.

The **first floor** houses all the smaller pieces. Going round in a clockwise direction, you work your way through the prehistoric eras, Bronze Age, Iron Age, Greek, Roman and Byzantine periods to the Arab Muslim era. The quality and beauty of the artefacts from all these periods is really stunning, but perhaps most breathtaking of all is the vast wealth of Bronze Age pieces from Byblos.

Particularly striking are the hundreds of gilded bronze sticklike figurines with their distinctive Egyptian style peaked hats found in the Temple of the Obelisks. Note also the beautifully fashioned solid gold axes. It is thought these were presented as to Reshef, the Amoritic god of war and destruction and his consort, the goddess Anat in order to secure their blessings for the continued cutting of the cedar forests. The fact that they are solid gold is an indication of how important these trees were to the wealth of Byblos. Similarly, the jewellery and weapons from the tombs of two Amoritic (early second millennium BC) princes of Byblos, Abi Shemou and Ip Shemou Abi show the extremely high levels of skill and craftsmanship which were applied to making such ceremonial offerings.

Around the National Museum

Beirut Hippodrome and Residence des Pins
① *T01-632 515, www.beiruthorseracing.com, racing takes place every Sun at 1230 during Sep-Jun, and every Sat at 1330 during Jul-Aug.*
At the turn of the century the Ottoman rulers of Lebanon granted a concession for the building of a race track, casino/private club and public gardens in a section of the large pine forest that then still existed to the south of Beirut. However, it was not until after the

fall of the Ottomans in the First World War that a member of the prestigious Sursock family established a race track here. During the civil war the hippodrome fell into disuse, but racing started up again soon afterwards.

The **Residence des Pins** ① *closed to visitors*, the impressive Ottoman-period building just to the west of the race track, was originally intended as the casino/private club, but it was leased instead to the French and used as the ambassador's residence. When the lease ran out, the French obtained ownership of it in exchange for other buildings belonging to them. During the civil war it was badly damaged by tank fire, but afterwards was fully restored and serves once again as the ambassador's residence.

Beit Beirut

① *Corner of Rue de Damas and Ave Independence, due to be opened to the public in 2013.*
A wonderful example of typical neo-Ottoman architecture, the beautiful old Barakat building suffered heavily during the civil war. With its prominent position along the Green Line, this once grand structure became a favoured sniper spot and the distinctive ochre-coloured stones soon became riddled with bullets.

Left to slowly decay for years, the Barakat building is now being restored to serve as a new cultural space for the city. Known as Beit Beirut, the building will include a museum dedicated to the history of the city.

West Beirut

The **Hamra** district emerged as the new financial and commercial centre of Beirut during the civil war and this vibrant district is still a hub for visitors with its excellent cafés, restaurants, shops and a good selection of hotels and services. It is not exactly picturesque and there is nothing really to 'see' as such, but it is buzzing with life.

Rue Hamra, running east-west, forms the main thoroughfare. From here you can explore the rough grid pattern of streets surrounding it and shop, dine and snack to your heart's content. Although practically all the buildings in Hamra are modern and rather ugly, here and there you can see the odd few dating from the French Mandate period; isolated reminders of a more elegant past. Heading down towards the **Corniche** along **Rue John Kennedy** and **Rue Omar ed-Daouk** you pass a number of these peeping out incongruously from among the modern tower blocks, including the old French embassy building. On Rue Omar ed-Daouk you can also see the derelict remains of the old **Holiday Inn** building. Opened in 1974 this hotel was for one year the favoured haunt of holidaying jet-setters to the city, symbolizing all that was glamorous about this Mediterranean hot-spot. Due to its prime position along the Green Line, at the outbreak of civil war in 1975 the Holiday Inn was one of the first buildings to be taken over by the militias. Now surrounded by shiny new high-rises and hotels, the bullet-pocked exterior of this empty shell is a stark reminder of the chaos and suffering of the civil war.

American University of Beirut

① *Rue Bliss, the main entrance is just to the east of the intersection with Rue Jeanne d'Arc.*
The AUB was first established in 1866 and named at that time the Syrian Protestant College. Founded by the American Protestant missionary Daniel Bliss, it was one of several foreign educational establishments that were opened following the advent of direct European involvement in the affairs of Lebanon in 1860. Others included the Beirut Women's College, likewise founded in 1860 and also in West Beirut (it became

Beirut University College and is now the Lebanese American University), and the University of St Joseph, founded in 1874 and located in East Beirut (still functioning under the same name). The AUB gained a reputation over the years as perhaps the most prestigious university in the Middle East and today it remains an exclusive, much sought-after (and extremely expensive) place to study. It continued to function throughout the civil war, remaining largely unscathed (notwithstanding the kidnap and murder of various members of its staff and a car bomb in 1991, which destroyed College Hall, the original building of the college founded by Bliss). The extensive grounds here, spreading down the hillside toward the Mediterranean, provide a wonderful oasis of leafy green tranquillity – a world away from the congestion and noise outside.

② West Beirut

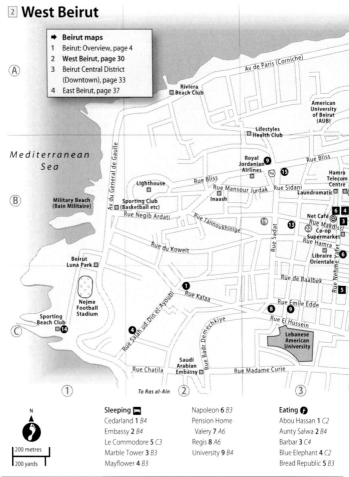

➤ Beirut maps
1 Beirut: Overview, page 4
2 West Beirut, page 30
3 Beirut Central District (Downtown), page 33
4 East Beirut, page 37

Sleeping ⌂		Eating 🍴
Cedarland 1 B4	Napoleon 6 B3	Abou Hassan 1 C2
Embassy 2 B4	Pension Home	Aunty Salwa 2 B4
Le Commodore 5 C3	Valery 7 A6	Barbar 3 C4
Marble Tower 3 B3	Regis 8 A6	Blue Elephant 4 C2
Mayflower 4 B3	University 9 B4	Bread Republic 5 B3

N
200 metres
200 yards

The **AUB Archaeological Museum** ⓘ *www.aub.edu.lb, Mon-Fri 0900-1700 during term time only, free,* houses an interesting collection of artefacts which have been gathered from around the wider Middle East region as well as from Lebanon itself. The emphasis is very much on the prehistoric and ancient periods up until Roman and early Byzantine times; stone implements of the Palaeolithic, Mesolithic and Neolithic periods; varied examples of the pottery styles/techniques of Mesopotamia and Egypt during the fifth and fourth millenniums BC; Sumerian administrative tablets from the kingdom of Ur; pottery, jewellery, figurines and fertility goddesses of the second and third millenniums BC from the Euphrates region of North Syria and from Phoenician coastal sites such as Byblos; the strikingly more sophisticated later Phoenician fertility goddesses and figurines of the Middle Iron Age (900-600 BC); and

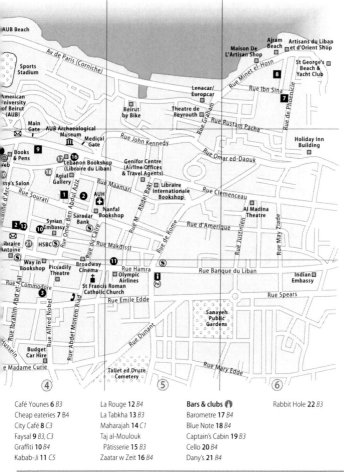

Hellenistic, Roman and Byzantine artefacts, including coins reaching up to the Umayyad period. Although many of the artefacts are very impressive, the labelling is unfortunately rather patchy and no attempt has been made at interpretive explanations of the displays.

The Corniche

Running the full length of West Beirut's northern and western seafront is the Corniche. This is where Beirutis come to exercise, socialize, enjoy the sunset and generally 'see and be seen' and a stroll here in the evening provides perfect people-watching opportunities.

Following it west, the Corniche proper starts from its junction with **Rue Minet el-Hosn** (opposite the Hard Rock Café and McDonald's). The first stretch passes through an area known as **Ain el-Mreisse** after the spring and tiny fishing bay located there (the entrance to the bay passes under the road, so you must cross over to see inside).

Further on is the **AUB 'beach'** (see page 48) and the university grounds stretching up the hill on the opposite side of the road, followed by the flashy Riveria hotel complete with its own private beach club/marina. A little further on the road swings south following the coastline. The small headland here is a particularly popular fishing spot. To the south, the military-only Bain Militaire is followed by a cluster of restaurants, cafés and private beach clubs (see listings, as above), a couple of the latter are just behind the wonderfully retro **Luna Park** fairground, dominated by a large Ferris wheel, and the football stadium.

The road then climbs steeply up to the cliffs that mark this stretch of the coast, known as Raouche, now an area of residential apartments, cafés, restaurants and brightly lit fast food outlets. Just beyond the cliffs, the famous **Pigeon Rocks** rise from the sea, two tall pillars of rock with arches hollowed through them at their bases by the action of the sea. During summer small boats ply the short trip from the shore to the rocks for you to admire them up close. Continuing south, the road descends, down to a long stretch of sand beach, known as **Rafiq Hariri beach** which is open to the public and has no entrance fee.

Beirut Central District (Downtown)

The city centre was largely destroyed during the civil war. Once a thriving financial and commercial centre of offices, hotels, cafés and markets, the entire heart of Beirut was smashed and devastated by the endless rounds of fighting. After the civil war it became the scene of one of the largest urban redevelopment projects in the world with many of the grand old Ottoman and French Mandate buildings painstakingly restored to their former glory. Some of the area (particularly around Place d'Etoile) has been fully pedestrianized, making it a quiet oasis away from the rest of the city.

Background

The redevelopment of the BCD is all the work of **Solidere** (or Société Libanaise pour le Développement et la Reconstruction du Centre-Ville de Beyrouth), formed in 1994 by the late Lebanese prime minister Rafiq Hariri. The primary objective of this private real estate company was to reconstruct the old downtown area of central Beirut in accordance with a government-approved master plan. The highly ambitious and ongoing scheme involves the redevelopment of 180 ha of land including over 60 ha of landfill reclaimed from the sea.

The single greatest obstacle to initiating a redevelopment project on such a large scale was the complex web of local land/property ownership and tenancy rights that existed within the area. In all, more than 40,000 active property owners were involved, while in one celebrated case it was revealed that 4750 people held ownership or tenancy rights to a single plot of land in the souqs. To get around this problem, all those with property rights of one sort or another were given shares in Solidere, amounting to a total value of US$1.17 billion, this being the estimated total value of private real estate in the BCD. In addition, outside investors were allowed to buy shares in the company to a value of US$650 million.

Solidere is responsible for carrying out all infrastructure works (roads, tunnels, bridges, public squares, gardens, etc), and also for treating the landfill on the reclaimed land and developing the sea defences and two associated marinas. In the historic core of the district (centred on Place d'Etoile), it has restored more than 250 Ottoman and French Mandate period buildings in an effort to preserve as much of the historic core of the city in its original form and layout as possible.

The redevelopment of the whole of the centre of the city presented archaeologists with a unique excavation opportunity. Remains from every period of occupation from the Canaanite period onwards were uncovered, and provisions were included in the master plan to preserve as much as possible of these remains in the form of archaeological gardens within the centre.

However, perhaps inevitably for an undertaking of this size, the project has drawn a great deal of criticism. Former property owners in the project area have claimed that the real value of land and property has been massively underestimated, describing Solidere as having pulled off the "biggest land-grab in history". At the same time, the differing

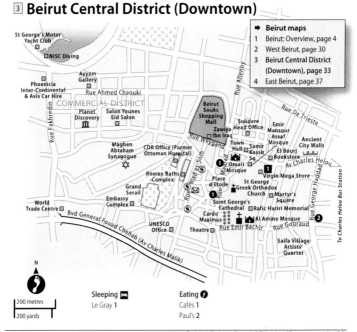

3 **Beirut Central District (Downtown)**

priorities of archaeologists keen to uncover and preserve as much as possible, and developers impatient to get on with the job of rebuilding the city centre, have led at times to tensions and even hostilities.

Smaller concerns include the lack of recreational facilities here, which would bring some life to the area. For the most part, the new BCD consists of high-end shops and office blocks that don't exactly bring the Beruitis thronging to the centre. On the outskirts of the centre (especially between the Intercontinental Phoenicia Hotel and the Beirut Souks) the area is still a massive construction zone, with cranes dominating the skyline, huge billboard fences covering whole blocks and advertising new apartment complexes, and the steady thump of concrete mixers echoing in the air. It is estimated that the entire finished plan won't be completed for another 30 years.

Place d'Etoile

Place d'Etoile and the streets radiating from it have been completely restored. Thought to stand on the site of the forum of the Roman city, this area was laid out in its present form by the French, with the north-south Rue Maarad being modelled on the Rue de Rivoli in Paris. Today, the architecture is striking, combining the quiet grace and elegance of restored Ottoman and French Mandate period buildings with the loud modernity of glass and steel office blocks. All along **Rue Maarad** and the surrounding streets are street-side cafés, fancy restaurants and expensive boutiques, which are just as at home here as they would be in Paris or Rome. This area is completely closed off to traffic, creating a surreally tranquil bubble right in the heart of the city. The best time to visit is during the early evening when Place d'Etoile and the surrounding streets come alive with local families utilizing the car-free streets for strolling and impromptu games of football. At other times the entire area can seem quite dead and soulless.

Grand Serail and Roman baths

On an area of higher ground to the west of Place d'Etoile, overlooking the old centre of Beirut, is the **Grand Serail**. This was built in 1890 and acted both as a barracks and the seat of the Ottoman government. Following independence it served as the Ministry of Interior. The building now houses the Council of Ministers and the prime minister's offices and is surrounded by heavy security. The smaller building immediately to the north of it was the Ottoman military hospital and now houses the Council for Development and Reconstruction (CDR), responsible for coordinating these activities at a national level.

Between the Grand Serail and Rue Riad es-Solh there is a long, narrow area of excavations where the remains of a **Roman baths** complex have been uncovered, preserved today as an archaeological 'garden'. The three rooms identified as the *caldarium, tepidarium* and *frigidarium* can be clearly discerned, along with the under-floor *hypocaust* (or heating system) consisting of raised floors supported on miniature pillars of discs. The channels cut into the surrounding bedrock in order to direct the flow of water can also be made out, along with a huge stone basin and traces of mosaics.

Just west of the Grand Serail, among a redeveloped area of presently empty new office blocks and apartment buildings that remains cordoned off to traffic due to its close proximity to the Serail is the **Maghen Abraham Synagogue**. The synagogue has been fully restored (although it isn't open to the public) and is one of the last reminders of Beirut's once vibrant Jewish community.

Beirut Souk (old souqs area)

At its north end, Rue Riad es-Solh intersects with the east-west Rue Weygand. To the north of Rue Weygand is what used to be the old souqs area and is now the exceedingly glamorous Beirut Souks shopping arcade where dressed-to-the-nines Beirutis come to browse the high-end shops and foreign clothing outlets.

Excavations have revealed that a market and complex of artisans' workshops existed here even from pre-Hellenistic times. Traces of Ottoman silk workshops, as well as Mamluk potteries and glass-blowing workshops were found, along with late Roman and Byzantine houses and shops, often with elaborate mosaic floors. Rue Weygand has in fact been shown to follow almost exactly the line of the Roman *decumanus*, while Souq Tawile ('Long Souq') also existed on this alignment from the Hellenistic period.

On the edge of the souqs area, immediately opposite the intersection of Rue Riad es-Solh and Rue Weygand, is the **Zawiye Ibn Iraq**, a small domed sanctuary dating from 1517 and the only Mamluk-period monument to survive in Beirut. Attributed to a Sufi religious authority named Ibn Iraq al-Dimashqi, it is thought to have served as a *zawiye*, or Sufi religious school. Along the west side of the souqs area there are traces of the medieval walls which once surrounded the old city. These have also been preserved in an archaeological 'garden'.

Omari Mosque

Heading east along Rue Weygand, on the south side of the road, is the Omari Mosque (or Grand Mosque), originally built in the mid-12th century by the Crusaders as the Church of St John the Baptist (on the site of an earlier Byzantine church which was itself built on the foundations of the Roman temple of Jupiter). In 1291, after the Mamluks had finally driven the Crusaders from Beirut for the last time, it was converted into a mosque.

Samir Kassir Square

Further east along the same street is a tiny landscaped square dominated by a statue of Samir Kassir; an outspoken journalist who was killed by a car bomb on 2 June 2005. A leading vocal critic of Syrian intervention within Lebanon, Kassir's murder is most often attributed to Syrian or pro-Syrian factions. The movingly simple tribute, which lays just a stone's throw from the An Nahar newspaper building where he once worked, is a fitting constant reminder of the dangers journalists in Lebanon face when daring to expose the truth. Just to the right of the statue are two quotes. Before the death of Rafiq Hariri, Kassir devoted much of his writing to condemning Solidere's redevelopment of Downtown and what he saw as the reckless destruction of the city. The first quote, in French, refers to this, translating as "Beirut, outward in its wealth, the city that is also outward in its ruins." The second, more poignant, quote in Arabic is his rallying cry to the Lebanese, written just after the murder of Hariri: "Return to the streets, dear comrades, and you will return to clarity."

Solidere information centre

ⓘ *In the grid of pedestrian streets to the north of Rue Weygand, Mon-Fri 0900-1800, free.*
The Solidere information centre boasts a huge and elaborate scale model of the BCD, which gives an excellent overview of the area and the controversial and ongoing redevelopment, as well as more detailed scale models of different areas, and even individual buildings.

St George's Cathedral

To the southeast of Place d'Etoile, on Rue Emir Bechir, before you reach Martyr's Square, is the Maronite Cathedral of St George. Heavily damaged during the war, it has been completely restored to its former glory. In its present form it dates from 1890, though it stands on the site of an older Maronite church built during the early 18th century. The towering façade, which is modelled on the Santa Maria Maggoria in Rome, is extremely imposing.

The interior, with its richly decorated ceiling and vast expanses of marble, is both lavish and yet at the same time somehow austere. Particularly striking is the wooden dome-topped structure that stands over the altar, supported on four massive wooden columns carved into twisting muscle-like corkscrews and topped by ornate Corinthian capitals. Behind it, on the wall of the apse, is a large painting of St George slaying the dragon. The cathedral has a basement of cavernous Ottoman barrel vaults which served as a storage and inventory centre for the archaeologists who worked so hard to rescue what they could of Beirut's past before it headed briskly into the future.

Immediately to the left of the cathedral as you face it, a number of re-erected columns mark the **Cardo Maximus** of the Roman city. The whole area surrounding the cathedral to the north was the focus of intensive excavations that have uncovered a large portion of the Roman market area and the remains of a number of important buildings.

Martyrs' Square and around

Although not much to look at (just a bare area of gravel really), Martyrs' Square is Lebanon's most famous congregation point and was the social focal point of old Beirut. This is where the famous Lebanese singer Fayrouz performed in 1994, in a concert that embodied the re-emerging peace and unity of the city. This is also where an approximate one million Lebanese converged on 14 March 2005 to commemorate the one month anniversary of Rafiq Hariri's death and protest against Syrian interference in the country.

Popularly known in Arabic as 'Al Bourj' (literally 'tower'), after a medieval watchtower that once stood at its southern end, it was later known as the 'Place des Cannons', when a huge cannon was set up here in 1772 during a brief occupation of the city by the Russian fleet of Catherine the Great. The name Martyrs' Square dates from the execution here of the leaders of the rebellion against Ottoman rule in 1840. A statue commemorating the martyrs stands in the square. During the civil war the square lay right on the Green Line; the statue was riddled with bullet holes but remained standing, becoming a poignant symbol of the city's suffering. It was restored after the war (but the bullet holes have been left intact) and returned to its original place.

Towering over the square on its western side is the modern **Al Amine mosque**, more commonly called the Rafiq Hariri mosque. Just to the side is the memorial to Rafiq Hariri himself.

Heading east from Martyrs' Square along Avenue Charles Helou, if you look over the north side of the avenue, you can see below you traces of the ancient **Canaanite and Phoenician city walls**. In the corner, by the point where the avenue crosses over Rue George Haddad, are the foundations of a later circular tower.

East Beirut

Rue de Damas marks the boundary between East and West Beirut; the various districts of East Beirut extending south up the hillside from the main port area. Along with Hamra, this is one of the main nightlife areas, with Gemmayze and Monot in particular packed full of restaurants, cafés, bars and clubs. Unlike West Beirut, it has also managed to retain far more of its Ottoman and French Mandate architecture, giving a taste of what the city was like before it was overtaken by developers. The most striking example of the opulent architecture of the late Ottoman period can be seen in the Sursock Museum building and in a number of the other houses along Rue Sursock.

Sursock Museum

ⓘ *Rue Sursock, T01-334133. Closed at time of research; it is due to be opened again in 2012.*
The strikingly elegant building in which this privately run museum is housed is one of

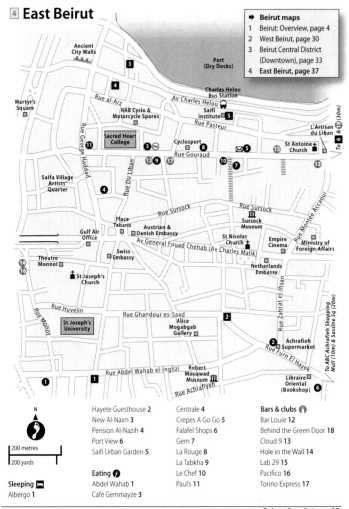

▣ East Beirut

➡ **Beirut maps**
1 Beirut: Overview, page 4
2 West Beirut, page 30
3 Beirut Central District (Downtown), page 33
4 East Beirut, page 37

N

200 metres
200 yards

Sleeping 🛏
Albergo **1**

Hayete Guesthouse **2**
New Al-Naim **3**
Pension Al-Nazih **4**
Port View **6**
Saifi Urban Garden **5**

Eating 🍴
Abdel Wahab **1**
Café Gemmayze **3**

Centrale **4**
Crepes A Go Go **5**
Falafel Shops **6**
Gem **7**
La Rouge **8**
La Tabkha **9**
Le Chef **10**
Paul's **11**

Bars & clubs 🍸
Bar Louie **12**
Behind the Green Door **18**
Cloud 9 **13**
Hole in the Wall **14**
Lab 29 **15**
Pacifico **16**
Torino Express **17**

several to be found around this affluent quarter of Christian East Beirut, but is of special interest in that it is open to the public. Built in 1902, it was dedicated as a museum on the death of its owner Nicolas Ibrahim Sursock in 1952 and since then has been maintained by the Sursock family as a museum (or, more accurately, a gallery of contemporary art). There is a small permanent exhibition that's supplemented by annual retrospective, foreign and other exhibitions. As well as being worth a visit simply to see the building, the exhibitions give an interesting insight into contemporary Lebanese art.

Robert Mouawad Private Museum
ⓘ *Corner of Rue Achrafieh and Rue Baroudi, T01-980970, Tue-Sun 0900-1700, 9000 LBP.*
The passionate collector Henri Pharaon spent a lifetime amassing this eclectic assortment of ceramics, antiques, art and typical Arabic craftwork inside his grand European-style villa known as the Pharaon Palace. After his death Robert Mouawad turned the residence into a museum where the wonderful clash of mostly Eastern decoration and mostly Western architecture is now spectacularly displayed.

Outside the central city

Cilicia museum
ⓘ *Antelias highway; the LCC No 6 bus travels via the Antelias highway on its way to Byblos, get off the bus once you're on the highway at the second road overpass, directly before the Coolrite building, the Holy See of Cilicia compound is 2 blocks up on the right-hand side of the road (you can see the church steeples from the overpass), Tue-Sun 0900-1500.*
Since 1930, after the destruction of the Monastery of St Sophia of Sis near present-day Adana in Turkey, this rather mundane location, on the main highway heading north out of Beirut, has been home to the Holy See of Cilicia, the seat of the Armenian Apostolic Church. Inside the complex (to the left of the entry) is the beautiful and engrossing Cilicia museum, which contains an incredible collection of religious artefacts. The museum is well worth a visit as much for the story behind the artefacts displayed as the items themselves. Much of what is displayed here was what the monks of the Monastery of St Sophia of Sis could salvage and then smuggle out of Turkey, with great risk, on their long walk overland into Syria.

Beirut listings

For Sleeping and Eating price codes and other relevant information, see pages 9-10.

🌙 Sleeping

Beirut *p21, maps p30, p33 and p37*
Accommodation is, in general, expensive. Unless you're in the top-end bracket of the market, don't expect your hotel room to come with all the bells and whistles attached. The price ranges for the hotels below are based on high-season (Jul-Aug) official full room rates, but even in mid-Aug discounts and special offers are sometimes offered if you book through hotel websites. It's always worth reserving your room as all the decent hotels tend to be booked out constantly. It's worth remembering that outside of the high season most of the city's mid-range and some of the top-end hotels drop their prices substantially and it's not unheard of to be able to get 30-40% off the price of your room during quiet periods.

Luxury hotels mostly congregate around Hamra, the BCD (Downtown), along the Corniche and in Achrafieh. Mid-range accommodation is based in Hamra, which means you're in prime position, right in the thick of the action. We've included the best of the city's budget choices, but if you're really down to your last pennies there are more budget hotels around the Port Area just off Av Charles Helou. Most deal mainly in beds for migrant workers, but they're used to backpackers wandering in. If you're a single female traveller on a budget it's safer to stick to the options listed below.

Beirut's more expensive hotels all charge a hefty service and government tax on top of the room rate. This has been included in the prices below. All rooms come with attached bathroom as standard unless otherwise stated.
$$$$ Albergo, Rue Abdel Wahab el-Inglizi, Achrafieh, T01-339797, www.albergobeirut. com. Set in a beautifully restored Ottoman-period mansion; gorgeous lamps, colourful carpets, modern art and antiques all mix and mingle beautifully, creating a totally individual look to each of the high-ceilinged rooms. It's a taste of the opulent days gone by, but with modern luxuries. By far Beirut's most special hotel experience. Restaurant, rooftop terrace with swimming pool and bar. Recommended.
$$$$ Le Commodore, Rue Commodore, Hamra, T01-350400, www. lecommodorehotel.com. The foreign journalists that stayed at the legendary Commodore during the civil war wouldn't recognize the place these days. Now part of the Meridien chain, this old dame of the Hamra scene (famous for managing to stay open in the midst of total bedlam) is now a classy top-end hotel. Well-appointed and comfortable rooms come with all the usual mod cons and are tastefully decorated. There are also lovely personal touches, which give the place a homely feel. Restaurants, bars, shops and swimming pool all on site.
$$$$ Le Gray, Martyr's Sq, Downtown, T01-971111, www.campbellgrayhotels.com. Beirut's new kid on the block in the luxury hotel market has been causing quite a stir. The hotel oozes classy contemporary chic with its fresh modern interiors warmed up by clever splashes of coloured textiles and fabrics. Le Gray is 'the' place to stay here in the city, and the rooms are, as you'd expect, equipped with all the latest gadgets and technology. The bathrooms are fit for a princess with their spacious walk-in showers and their own TVs. Commanding views over the surrounding countryside, the rooftop swimming pool, with its swish sun terrace, is the perfect retreat from the chaos of the city. Fabulous restaurants, spa, bar, Wi-Fi.
$$$ Hayete Guesthouse, Rue Furn El-Hayek (1st floor, above 'Frida' restaurant), Achrafieh, T70-271530, www.hayete-guesthouse.com. For something completely different, this quirkily cool guesthouse right in the heart

of Achrafieh has just 5 rooms on offer (fan and a/c, some with/without bathroom), all individually decorated. It's a charmingly funky place with lashings of character, high ceilings, some of the original intricate floor tiles still in place, gleaming bathrooms and a cute communal balcony perfect for lazing around on. A wonderfully intimate and arty alternative. Breakfast included, Wi-Fi, reserve as far in advance as possible as it's often booked out. Recommended.

$$$ Mayflower, Rue Nehme Yafet, Hamra, T01-340680, www.mayflowerbeirut.com. Although rather blandly decorated, the decent-sized rooms (some with balcony) here are comfortably appointed with minibar, a/c and satellite TV and are sparkling clean. Bathrooms have been recently renovated and are snazzily modern. It's in a great position just down from busy Rue Hamra. Overall, a solid choice, though staff could try to be a bit more interested. Across the road is the **Napoleon Hotel** which offers pretty much the same deal. Pub, restaurant, small rooftop swimming pool.

$$ Cedarland, Rue Omar Ben Abdul Aziz, Hamra, T01-340233. An excellent central location for a hotel in this price range. You don't get much, but the large clean rooms come with a/c and satellite TV as standard and some have balconies attached. The bathrooms could do with an update but they're decently sized. For this price we're not complaining. The downstairs coffee shop is a nice added touch.

$$ Embassy, Rue Makdissi, Hamra, T01-340814, www.embassyhotellebanon.com. The Embassy exudes old-fashioned, cosy charm. The clean rooms (a/c, minibar, fridge, satellite TV) are decked out in enough frills and chintz to make your grandma proud and most have dinky balconies that look out onto the inner garden rather than the street. The inner garden is a lovely place to escape the chaos outside and the staff here are a genuinely welcoming bunch.

$$ Hotel Libanais, T03-513766, www.hotelibanais.com. For those who'd prefer a more intimate option than a hotel, this small company offers you a glimpse of Lebanese life with 2 B&B accommodation options in the city. It's a chance to experience the friendly and welcoming Lebanese in their own homes. As well as Beirut, Hotel Libanais has B&B accommodation throughout the country. Reservations (at least 48 hrs' notice) are required. Check their website for details.

$$ Marble Tower, Rue Makdissi, Hamra, T01-354586, www.marbletowerhotel.com. This welcoming choice has small but functional rooms that come with balcony, a/c, satellite TV and bathrooms that are a tad on the squashy side. The friendly staff are a definite bonus as is the central location.

$$ Pension Al-Nazih, just off Av Charles Helou, Port Area, T01-564868, www.pensionalnazih.com. This cute place, not far from Martyr's Sq, pulls the punters in with its cheerful clean rooms and lively communal area. The doubles here have a/c, satellite TV and private bath while the 5-bed dorms (US$17), which share decent communal bathrooms, have fan and satellite TV. The only downside is the surly day manager who definitely isn't the host with the most. Save all your questions for the lovely and on-the-ball evening manager. Recommended.

$$ Port View, Rue Al Nahr (just off Rue Gouraud), Gemmayze, T01-567500, www.portviewhotel.com. A friendly place just a short stroll from the Rue Gouraud bar scene. The airy rooms (a/c, satellite TV) are large and clean though sparsely furnished. The downside is the bathrooms, which are slightly run down and a bit of a tight squeeze.

$$ Regis, just off Rue Ibn Sina, Hamra, T01-361845, www.regishotel-lb-com. A short stroll from the Corniche, the friendly Regis is a home away from home. Upstairs the sparsely furnished rooms (a/c, satellite TV) are made bright and cheerful by colourful bedding. Downstairs it's more living room than foyer, with book exchange, squashy sofas, free Wi-Fi and the obliging manager Mazer, who is always ready to dish out information and advice. Highly recommended.

$$ University, Rue Bliss, Hamra, T01-365391. A clean, simple and safe place to rest your head; the rooms here are nothing special but do come with a/c and satellite TV. Unfortunately competition for rooms is stiff due to this place being booked up by AUB students during term time, but during term holidays you should get a room no problems. Wi-Fi.

$ CYC Guesthouse, Shatila Palestinian refugee camp (ask your service taxi driver to take you to Shatila and drop you at Sabre Hmadeh intersection; if you ring ahead the CYC staff can meet you here), T03-974672, www.cycshatila.org. This wonderful initiative was set up as an income-generating project for the Shatila Children and Youth Centre (CYC), which runs after-school activities, tutoring and training programs for the youths living in the camp. Based in the same building as the CYC offices, the guesthouse has basic rooms (dorm beds only – US$10), with a communal kitchen (fridge, washing machine, cooker) available for guests' use and a cheerful lounge with TV. There are absolutely no luxuries here, but it's all clean, incredibly friendly and is a wonderful opportunity for visitors to find out more about Palestinian life within the camps. There are copious opportunities to work as a volunteer here.

$ New Al-Naim, just off Av Charles Helou, Port Area, T01-587375. Under new management, who are really endeavouring to please, the Al-Naim could be Beirut's new penny-pinching winner soon. The rooms are as basic as they come (fan only), but they're clean and flooded with light. The 13 rooms share 6 bathrooms between them so there isn't too much waiting around for a shower. The dorms (US$10) are men only, but single female travellers should be able to bargain down the price of the double with a bit of friendly haggling. A safe and friendly choice for those tight on their pennies.

$ Pension Home Valery, 2nd Floor, Saab Building, Rue Ibn Sina, Ain Mreisse, T01-362169. Probably the cheapest doubles in town are offered here (and there's even cheaper dorm accommodation too). As you'd expect, it's completely frills-free, with the fan-only rooms all sharing bathrooms, but it's clean and fabulously located just off the Corniche. It's tricky to find as there's no signage out front. Ring to ask directions and when you get to Rue Ibn Sina ask directions from one of the local shop owners, everyone seems to know where it is.

$ Saifi Urban Gardens, Rue Pasteur (behind Coral Petrol St), Gemmayze, T01-562509, www.saifigardens.com. Hands down the best budget choice in town, the newly opened and wonderfully friendly Saifi Urban Gardens manages to be a tranquil oasis while still being in the thick of the action. The high-ceilinged rooms are airy, bright and decently sized and have a fresh modern twist. All rooms come with a/c and fan and even the 6-bed dorms (US$18), which are the roomiest in the city, have their own private bathrooms. Guests have free Wi-Fi and access to a washing machine, there's a great common area, breakfast is included and there are excellent discounted rates for long stays. Highly recommended.

🍴 Eating

Beirut *p21, maps p30, p33 and p37*
If you've been hanging around the Middle East for a while, you'll probably descend on Beirut's dining scene like a thirsty man coming in from the desert. And if you've just flown in, you're going to be amazed at how cosmopolitan this city's restaurant-life is. Not only is this city home to some of the best Levantine cuisine in the region but, if you're feeling like a break from meze and other Arab staples, you'll have no problems tracking down restaurants specializing in French, Italian, Japanese, Indian, Chinese, Thai or basically any other world cuisine. The average cost of a meal out in Beirut is around US$20 and portions tend to be on the generous side, so it's comparatively cheaper than eating out in many European cities.

If you're on a budget though, all this indulging your tastebuds doesn't come cheap. Luckily the city is full of hole-in-the-wall style bakeries, falafel and *shawarma* stands, where you can easily fill up for 5000 LBP or less. Excellent local chain outlets such as **Kabab-Ji** and **Barbar** dish up brilliant *shawarma*, while **Faysal** does a whole range of budget pastries and pizza and is open around the clock. A good place for cheap eats in Hamra is along Rue Bliss, opposite the AUB, where dozens of budget eateries line the street. In Gemmayze there are also some great cheapies. Rue Gouraud has the great **Crepes A GoGo** by the post office, and there are a couple of good falafel stores on Rue Furn El Hayek, opposite the ABC shopping mall. A patisserie/gelato store worth hunting out is **Taj al-Moulouk** on Rue Bliss in Hamra. The gelato they do here is particularly delicious, the service is great and at only 1500 LBP a scoop you can afford to indulge.

The distinction between restaurant, café and bar is pretty fluid in Beirut: many of the restaurants merge into bars complete with thumping music and dancing later in the evening, while most of the bars serve food with menus sometimes as extensive (and as good) as that in a restaurant.

Centrale, Rue Mar Maroun, Saifi, T03-915925. Daily 2000-2430. If you're dying for a steak then this is the place to come. The French-inspired menu inside this architecturally designed modernist restaurant isn't cheap, but it really is dining in style, especially on a balmy summer night if you've bagged a table on the terrace. Top-notch food and a chance to peek at Beirut's glitterati. The bar here is also a high-class option. Reservations necessary.

Tawlet, ground floor, Chalhoub Building, Naher St, T01-442664. Mon-Fri 1300-1600, Sat 1200-1600. If you want to sample the best of Lebanese home cooking you really need to dine out at Tawlet. It offers up regional specialities from around the country with an ever-changing band of chefs from across Lebanon who come here to cook their area's special dishes. Hence the daily menu is always different. It's a foodie's dream and a fantastic way to sample Lebanon's array of cuisine. Recommended.

Abdel Wahab, Rue Abdel Wahab el-Inglizi, Monot, T01-200550. Daily 1200-2400. A great choice for sampling the typical Levantine cuisine this country is so famous for. If you can get a few people together, go crazy with the meze selection so you can check out as many of the dishes as possible.

Abou Hassan, Rue Salah ud-Din el-Ayoubi, Manara, T01-741725. Daily 0800-2200. Hidden away on a small street leading inland back towards Hamra and Ras Beirut, this small traditional Lebanese restaurant has a well-deserved reputation for serving excellent Arabic food at very reasonable prices. The pleasant atmosphere and friendly staff are a definite bonus. Recommended.

Aunty Salwa, Baalbaki Building, off Rue Abdel Aziz, Hamra, T01-749746. Mon-Sat 0900-1700. Incredibly friendly, this place serves up hearty home-style Lebanese dishes – the sort you don't find on the menu anywhere else. There's no traditional-style menu, just whatever choices are being cooked that day. Recommended.

Blue Elephant, Searock Hotel, Rue Salah ud-Din el-Ayoubi, Raouche, T01-788588. A good Thai restaurant with hilarious over-the-top decor (think waterfall and fish pond). The *chiang rai* (a spicy beef stir fry of beef, garlic and chilli, 15,000 LBP) and the *panaeng kai* (chicken and coconut curry, 14,000 LBP) are both delicious, while the *massaman* (slowly braised lamb, 20,000 LBP) is worth splashing out for. There are heaps of options for vegetarians here too. Recommended.

Gem, Mar Nicholas stairs, just off Rue Gouraud, Gemmayze. Daily 1800-late. This dinky restaurant/bar is an excellent place to start off a night in Gemmayze. There's a relaxed and casual vibe and a decent range of snack type starters and more filling mains. A great place to just come for a drink as well.

La Rouge, Rue Makdissi, Hamra and Rue Gouraud, Gemmayze, T01-353585. Daily 0900-late. This chic Parisian-style café has a French-inspired menu, friendly service and is a favourite among the ladies who lunch. The steak sandwich (served with caramelized onions, mushrooms and mustard sauce) is a winner at 16,000 LBP, and there's a whole range of salads and snacks, pizzas and sandwiches (8000-26,000 LBP). They also serve breakfast and it's a good option if you just want a decent cappuccino.

¶¶ La Tabkha, Rue Mahatma Ghandi, Hamra, T01-347346, and Rue Gouraud, Gemmayze, T01-579000. This brightly coloured little place does simple Lebanese, home-style cooking with a couple of different dishes that change daily (17,000 LBP). There's also an all vegetarian meze buffet (15,000 LBP) that allows you to try a bit of everything.

¶¶ Maharajah, next to the Sporting Beach Club, off Av du General de Gaulle, Ain El Mreisseh, T01-742275. Daily 1200-2400. Serving up generous portions of decent Indian cuisine, this restaurant has a great position looking over the Mediterranean. There are some excellently priced options. If you want to splash out, the spicy mutton madras (23,000 LBP) and the fish tikka (19,000 LBP) are both delicious. If you're an Indian-food fanatic, don't forget to ask for your meal 'spicy' rather than normal. Recommended.

¶ Le Chef, Rue Gouraud, Gemmayze, T01-445373. Mon-Sat 0700-2100. Welcome! Welcome! Welcome! This place is legendary for the hilarious antics of the owner who, if in the mood, booms out the word 'welcome' to you at least 20 times during the course of your meal. Yes, it's now a tourist trap and yes, the food can be so-so, but this unpretentious café is a cheerful and low-cost choice where you can eat for well less than US$10. Simple dishes (5000-8000 LBP) and meze (2000-6000 LBP) are all hearty and filling, and the hummus here is fantastic. A good fun, no-frills option. Recommended.

¶ Zaatar w Zeit, Rue Bliss, Hamra. Always packed with students from the nearby AUB, this local chain restaurant does its own delicious take on the staple *mannoushi* as well as offering all sorts of other pastry delights. Cheap, filling and tasty.

Cafés

Café culture is huge in Beirut and you'll find a good café on nearly every street corner. There are literally dozens of cafés in Hamra, especially along Rue Hamra and Rue Makdissi; all over the Achrafieh district; and in the Downtown area there are loads of places to put your feet up on the streets radiating out from Place d'Etoile.

Bread Republic, in an alleyway off Rue Hamra, Hamra. Daily 0730-2400. A very cool Hamra café favoured by Beirut's bohemian set and the perfect place to settle down for a few hours and write your journal or read a book. The inside is tiny but there is great outdoor seating that spreads across the narrow alleyway. The coffee is slightly ho-hum, but there are excellent lemonade, juices and cocktails. If you're peckish, the original menu uses all locally sourced and seasonal ingredients and there are imaginative options. They also bake their own range of speciality breads, Recommended.

Café Gemmayze, Rue Gouraud, Gemmayze. Daily 1000-late. This lovely little place is a Rue Gouraud institution. An excellent choice to sit back and puff on a *narghile*, especially in the evenings when they often have musicians playing traditional Lebanese music.

Café Younes, Rue Nehme, Hamra. Daily 0700-2400. You'll probably smell the tantalizing wafts of freshly ground coffee before you actually get here. Café Younes has been around since 1935 and is still going strong. This is a top place to put your feet up for an hour or so with a coffee, tea or one of Younes' delicious sandwiches.

City Café, Rue Sadat, Hamra. Daily 0700-2400. An oldie but a goody; City Café is a friendly joint with a devoted following of regulars who come here for the decent coffee, pastries and more substantial meals. An excellent choice for breakfast.

Graffiti, Rue Makdissi, Hamra. This funky café with its mauve and lime green decor is patronized by a fairly hip and young crowd. The cappuccino served here is damn good, and the comfy couches are great to lounge on. If you're feeling decadent try the oreo cookie milkshake (8500 LBP). The well-stocked bar makes it also a great place for an evening's drinking.

Paul's, Rue Gouraud, Gemmayze. This café is always crowded with locals who come here for the excellent coffee and great range of pastries and breads that are baked on site. The service is friendly and efficient and the menu is extensive if you're hungry. The only unfortunate side is that the outdoor terrace is blighted by the constant traffic and construction noise from the busy main road.

☊ Bars and clubs

Beirut *p21, maps p30, p33 and p37*
Bars

Beirut's nightlife is alive and kicking with something for everyone. The 'in' places change regularly, with fickle crowds migrating somewhere new at rapid speed. The main nightlife areas are Hamra, Monot and Gemmayze. The bars in Hamra tend to be more casual affairs and many lean towards having a bohemian air about them. Prices tend to be cheaper here as well. Monot nightlife is concentrated in a small area around Rue Monot. Gemmayze has a more classy nightlife scene, with lots of more upscale bars. The bars are strung out along Rue Gouraud and the small streets leading off it. No places really get going until after 2300.

A couple of things to note: many of the more upscale places (especially in Gemmayze) have cover charges, but you often won't be charged as you arrive. Instead you'll be charged on your final bill. Also, on bar menus all over Beirut (and Lebanon) you'll see 'Mexican beer' for sale. This is not a bottle of Corona, but a rather sickly concoction of almaza beer with lemon juice added to the glass and with the glass rim coated in salt. You'll either love it or hate it!

Barometre, Rue Makhoul, Hamra, T01-367229. Daily 1900-late. Immensely popular, Barometre is a hip spot where a cool mix of locals hang out for the great music (a blend of Arabic pop and Latin) and excellent food. They do a delicious range of meze options, so it's a good choice for a whole night of drinking, eating and dancing. If you want to get a seat, come here early as it gets jam-packed as the night progresses. Despite the lack of space, patrons break out their dancing moves later on in the evening and strut their stuff between the tables and chairs. A great, fun bar. Recommended.

Bar Louie, Rue Gouraud, Gemmayze, T01-575877. Daily 2000-late. This old timer is still going strong and, with its kicked-back atmosphere and live music, it's a lot more laid back than some of the other bars here.

Behind the Green Door, Rue Nahr, just off Rue Gouraud, Mar Mikhael, T01-565656. Daily 2000-late. Beirut does ostentatious well, and this bar, with its opulent draperies and decorations and patronized by the la-di-dah boys and girls of Beirut high society, sums it up pretty well. Absolutely brilliant for people-watching and seeing how the other half live. Dress up, and plan on it being an expensive night. Reservations necessary.

Captain's Cabin, Rue Makdissi, Hamra. Daily 1700-late. A totally unpretentious and dingy Hamra institution that gets packed out with a nice mix of university students and expats. You can play a game of pool or have a quiet drink at the bar. Recommended.

Cello, Rue Jeanne d'Arc, Hamra. Comfy sofas in muted pastels, friendly service and a great upstairs outdoor terrace surrounded with plants. They seem to play music at a couple of decibels lower than other Beiruti bars, so it's a fantastic choice if you want to have an evening of chatting rather than dancing. Serves up a decent enough menu of international cuisine if you're peckish.

Cloud 9, Rue Gouraud, Gemmayze, T01-566376. Daily 1900-late. A comfy, loungey type bar that does some cracking food as well. The crowd tends to lean to the 'young, beautiful and highly made-up' side and sipping cocktails is the name of the game.

Dany's, off Rue Makdissi, Hamra. Daily 0900-

late. With walls covered in graffiti, good music, friendly service and decently priced beer, Dany's is the 'in' bar for Hamra's arty set. It gets quite a squeeze in here later on so come before 2200 if you want to grab a table. Recommended.

Hole in the Wall, Monot Alley, Monot. Daily 1800-late. The sort of relaxed place you can easily spend an entire evening, Hole in the Wall's down-to-earth attitude is a great place for a few (or more) beers. The music is a tad loud, so don't plan on a deep and meaningful conversation with your friends, but apart from that it's a good solid choice.

Pacifico, next to Hole in the Wall, Monot Alley, Monot, T01-204446. Daily 1900-late. With a bit of Latin American style going on, popular Pacifico is a fun place for cocktails and dancing to the Cuban beats. If you want to eat (the Caribbean-inspired menu is delicious and there are lots of snacky type options), be sure to reserve a table as this place gets packed. Happy hour 1900-2000.

Rabbit Hole, Rue Makdissi, Hamra. Daily 1500-late. Anyone short of cash should make note of Rabbit Hole's daily happy hour, between 1700-2000, when cocktails (obviously on the watered-down side) only cost 3000 LBP. Apart from that, this itsy-bitsy bar is nothing special, but the cheap drinks make a good start to the night. A bottle of almaza is only 5000 LBP at all times, and there's a small menu of sandwiches and snacks to wash all that alcohol down with.

Torino Express, Rue Gouraud, Gemmayze. Daily 1200-late. During the day this teensy place is a good spot to grab a coffee in Gemmayze, while in the evening it turns into a friendly bar with a mixed bag of music and a nice crowd. A top spot though it can get ridiculously packed later on.

Clubs and live music

BO18, off Av Charles Helou (adjacent to the landmark Forum de Beyrouth), T01-580018. Thu-Sat 2100-late. BO18 (that's pronounced 'Bee Oh Eighteen') is Beirut's prime venue for debauchery and serious dancing action.

Housed in a massive underground bunker with black leather couches lining the walls, this place attracts a huge cross section of Beiruti clubbers, but definitely verges on the alternative side. The prime feature is the roof – it can be opened to let in fresh air – and this they do again, and again, and again as the night draws on. Hilarious, and completely ridiculous. Despite the location, overpriced drinks and the cover charge, this place is not to be missed if you're a clubber.

Blue Note, Rue Makhoul, Hamra, T01-743857. Mon-Sat 1200-late. Live music fans will love the changing line up of live jazz bands on Fri and Sat nights. There are sometimes blues and rock acts as well. It's an unpretentious joint with a decent dinner menu. A minimum charge applies on Fri and Sat nights.

Lab 29, Rue Gouraud, Gemmayze, T01-566969. Daily 1900-late. A very cool late-night venue that attracts a trendy crowd who like to lounge around on the couches between boogies to the overly loud music.

Sky Bar, Biel Pavillion, Downtown, T03-939191, www.sky-bar.com. Summer months only, Tue-Sun 2030-late. Beirut's most talked about venue, the roof terrace Sky Bar is the city's see-and-be-seen venue of choice on balmy summer evenings. With an exclusive reputation to keep up, this place charges a minimum rate of US$100 per person if you want to sit at a table (yes you did read that right) and you'll need to make a reservation beforehand. A slightly less wallet-bashing way to experience this place is to queue up for a place at the bar. Dress to impress.

🎭 Entertainment

Beirut *p21, maps p30, p33 and p37*
Children
Beirut Luna Park, Av du General de Gaulle. The original Beirut fairground, with funky dodgem cars and a retro ferris wheel.
Habtoorland, 15-min drive from central Beirut. Just off the Damascus highway, the signposted turning is 5 mins after Hazmieh. This massive Phoenician-styled theme park is

every child's dream. There's 27 rides to choose from, loads of restaurants and entertainment galore here. Just to top it off the amphitheatre here shows a laser show every evening.

Planet Discovery, Rue Omar ed-Daouk, Downtown, T01-980650. Mon-Thu 0900-1500, Fri-Sat 1000-1900. Described as a 'children's science museum', there are lots of different activities and interactive games for children here, from age 3 through to 15. There are puppet shows every Sat, while during the week there are organized programmes.

Cinema

The *Daily Star* newspaper has cinema listings.

Art Lounge, Karantina River Bridge, near Beirut Forum, Karantina, T03-997676, www.artlounge.net. Art-house and alternative films shown every Sun. See their website for details on what's screening.

Empire Sodeco, Sodeco Sq, Achrafieh, T01-616707. Popular multiplex showing all the latest Hollywood blockbusters.

Grand ABC, ABC Mall, Rue Achrafieh, Achrafieh, T01-209109. Always busy, this multiplex has 7-screens to choose from.

Galleries

Beirut's art scene is booming. There are dozens of small galleries around town exhibiting young emerging local artists as well as international names.

Agial, Rue Abdel Aziz, Hamra, www.agialart. com. Mon-Fri 1000-1800, Sat 1000-1400. A huge range of Middle Eastern artists are represented in this 2-levelled gallery. Upstairs is the permanent collection, while the ground floor plays host to a regular turn-over of exhibitions. One of the best places in town to check out the local art scene.

Alice Mogabgab, 1st floor, Karam Building, Rue Achrafieh, Achrafieh, www. alicemogabgabe.com. Mon-Fri 1030-1330 and 1500-1900, Sat 1030-1330. An impressive collection of modern art (both local and international) is on display here.

Art Lounge, Karantina River Bridge, near Beirut Forum, Karantina, www.artlounge.

net. This funky space focuses on young local artists and has a program of changing exhibitions. Also weekly cinema nights (see above) and various other cultural events.

Arts and Beyond, Sodeco Sq, Achrafieh, Mon-Fri 1100-1900, Sat 1100-1700. The work of 23 acclaimed Lebanese painters are hung here and much of the work can be bought.

Ayyam, ground floor, Beirut Tower, Corniche, Downtown, T70-535301. Mon-Sat 1000-2000. Opened in 2009, this gallery is dedicated to showcasing contemporary work by artists from all over the Arab world.

Theatres

Al Medina, Rue Clemenceau, Hamra, T01-753011. Has an ever-changing program of theatre, dance and other cultural productions. Tickets can be bought on site.

Monot, Rue University of St Joseph, adjacent to St Joseph's Church, Monot, T01-202422, www.usj.edu.lb. Wide variety of performances (dance, music and theatre).

⊕ Festivals and events

Beirut *p21, maps p30, p33 and p37*

May Spring Festival, a 5-day garden show event that turns the city's Hippodrome into a floral extravaganza.

Jun Fete de la Musique, began in Beirut in 1982, this is a celebration of world music that plays at various venues throughout the capital, and in the streets of Downtown, Hamra and Gemmayzeh. The festival takes place over the summer solstice.

Jun Gemmayze Stairs Art Festival, this wonderful local art carnival utilizes the length of the St Nicholas stairs, turning the entire stairway into a unique gallery space. It's an original and quirky way to bring art to the people and both international artists and complete amateurs can exhibit.

Jul-Aug Docudays, www.docudays.com, Beirut's international documentary festival shows a selection of international and local documentaries at various venues in the city.

Jul-Aug Beirut International Film Festival,

www.beirutfilmfoundation.org, one of the Middle East's premier film festivals; Beirut plays host to the best cinema offerings from across the globe.

Nov Beirut International Marathon, www.beirutmarathon.org, taking over the streets of Beirut, runners from all across the globe compete in this annual event.

⚙ Shopping

Beirut *p21, maps p30, p33 and p37*
Books
Beirut has some excellent bookshops. Most stock a wide range of books in English and French as well as Arabic, and a startling array of international magazines and newspapers (though prices aren't particularly cheap).
Books and Pens, Rue Jeanne d'Arc, Hamra. Not so many books, but stationery addicts will find this a brilliant place to browse and there's also a good selection of magazines.
El Bourj, ground floor of An Nahar Building, just off Martyr's Sq, Downtown. Fantastic collection of books on Lebanon and the Middle East.
Libraire Antoine, Rue Hamra, Hamra. An absolutely huge selection of international magazines and newspapers and downstairs there is a vast array of books in English and French, with Lebanese and Middle Eastern authors well represented and a decent politics/history section.
Libraire Oriental, Rue Hamra, Hamra. Large collection of books in English, French and Arabic, including a good range of fiction by Arabic authors. Also, coffee table books on Lebanon and travel books.
Virgin Megastore, Martyr's Sq, Downtown and ABC Mall, Achrafieh. The massive Virgin store carries a wide range of titles as well as lots of glossy magazines. The travel section here is the best in the city, the history and politics section is pretty good and the range of novels is excellent. The smaller branch in Achrafieh doesn't have as much choice.
Way Inn, Rue Hamra, Hamra. An eclectic mix of books, stationery and international magazines

and newspapers. There is a decent range of books focusing on Middle Eastern history and politics with some fiction thrown in.

Handicrafts, antiques and souvenirs
Compared to the souqs of Damascus and Aleppo in Syria, the prices of handicrafts in Beirut are high, but in general so is the quality. If you're planning on travelling on to Syria though, it's a better bet to leave your souvenir shopping until then.
There are numerous souvenir/antique shops in Hamra, along and in the streets radiating off Rue Hamra. In Achrafieh there are numerous antique shops, most of them specializing in elegant furniture and furnishings along the lines of reproduction Louis XIV items, but there are also lots of places selling smaller items such as jewellery. Rue Achrafieh is a good street to browse in. The artist's quarter of **Saifi village** is home to plenty of boutique gift stores.
Artisans du Liban et d'Orient, Rue Minet el-Hosn, Ain el-Mreisse. Mon-Fri 1000-1800, Sat 1000-1330. Interesting selection of handicrafts and local produce including hand-woven rugs, fabrics, glassware, soaps, spices and some books.
Hassan Maktabi & Sons, Av General de Gaulle, Raouche. Mon-Sat 0900-1800. A highly reputable carpet dealership with an absolutely huge selection of Central Asian carpets and *kilims* (Persian, Turkish, Caucasian and Nomadic).
Inaash, 1st floor, Bikhaazi and Cherif Building, off Rue Sidani, Hamra, www.inaash.org. Mon-Fri 0900-1400, Sat 0900-1300. Showroom for the work created by the women employed by the Association for Palestinian Embroidery in Lebanon. Employing over 450 female Palestinian refugees, this project not only provides the women with money but also makes sure that the traditional designs of Palestinian embroidery are kept alive.
L'Artisan du Liban, Rue Gouraud, Gemmayze. Mon-Fri 0930-1900, Sat 0930-1500. A large array of handmade traditional crafts, many with a modern twist.

Maison De L'Artisan, Rue Minet el-Hosn, Ain el-Mreisse. Mon-Sat 0930-2000. Large government-sponsored shop displaying a wide range of souvenirs and traditional handicrafts from all over Lebanon: ceramics, tapestries, woven rugs, silver jewellery, *narghiles*, pottery, metal-ware, cutlery, glassware, inlaid wood items, fabrics, etc.

Souk El-Tayeb, Sat 0900-1400 in Saifi village parking area, Downtown (BCD); Wed 1600-2000 in L3 parking area, ABC Mall, Achrafieh. Bringing the countryside to the city, Souk El-Tayeb gives farmers from all over Lebanon a platform to sell their products. An excellent range of organic produce is on display.

▲ Activities and tours

Beirut *p21, maps p30, p33 and p37*
Beach clubs
The term 'Beach Club' is something of a misnomer, since there are only a couple of real sand beaches in Beirut. For most Lebanese, however, the absence of any beach at their favourite beach club is neither here nor there. What's important is that it's a club, a private place for relaxing, socializing and enjoying a sense of exclusivity (though these days the majority are open to the public for a straightforward entrance fee). Be warned, turning up at most of these clubs without a tanned and toned body is verging on the subversive. Starting at St George's and following the coast west and then south, the main clubs are in the following order:

St George's Yacht Club, Rue Minet el-Hosn, T01-327 050. Mon-Fri 20,000 LBP, child 15,000 LBP; Sat-Sun 25,000 LBP, child 20,000 LBP. Formerly, this was a luxury hotel with its own private beach club and marina but, like most of the hotels and restaurants in this area, St George's was devastated during the civil war. The large hotel building still stands in a state of ruin (there is a long-standing legal battle between the owners and Solidere, with the latter claiming ownership of the land/sea frontage as part of the redevelopment area), but the adjoining

beach club and marina is as popular as ever amongst wealthy Beirutis. Facilities include a swimming pool, waterslide, children's play area, restaurant, three bars, a small marina for motor yachts, jet skis for hire and a privately run diving club. During the summer, evening entertainments are often laid on (singers, bands, dancing, etc).

Ajram Beach, Rue Minet el-Hosn. T01-374753, 10,000 LBP. The city's first women-only beach club is still going strong. Rather basic facilities compared to other clubs.

AUB Beach, Corniche, non-AUB students 10,000 LBP. Reached via a tunnel from the university grounds, this is a less well-maintained beach than others along the Corniche but a fun and friendly place to spend an afternoon sunbathing.

Riviera Beach Club, Corniche, T01-373210, Mon-Fri 30,000 LBP, Sat-Sun 40,000 LBP, child 25,000. Nicknamed 'silicone beach' for a reason, this highly prestigious beach club does nothing by halves, with swimming pool, health centre (with jacuzzi, sauna, massage and gym), as well as a restaurant and bar. This isn't the place for showcasing your old pair of boardies and tired flip flops.

Sporting Beach Club, Corniche, T01-742200, Mon-Sun 20,000 LBP. Strong family emphasis, with 2 large swimming pools and a children's pool, large concrete sunbathing area and steps down to the sea. Restaurants.

Rafiq Hariri Beach, to the south of Raouche heading down towards the Summerland and Coral Beach hotels, free public beach. As well as having a decent stretch of good sand that's kept relatively clean, a sectioned-off swimming area, snack bar and basic shower and changing facilities, this beach has the advantage of being open to the general public with no entrance fee required.

City tours
Walk Beirut, T70-156673, www.bebeirut. org/walk. Walk Beirut offers an in-depth insider's look at Beirut on an absorbing 4-hr wander through its streets. Led by recent university graduates, the walking tour

traverses the many diverse neighbourhoods that make up Lebanon's capital and allows visitors an eye-opening introduction to the complex history of this fascinating city. Tours (30,000 LBP) run on Wed, Sat and Sun and are all conducted in English. Check the website for the latest schedule and to book a place. Highly recommended. See page 40.

Diving
Calypso Diving Club, Movenpick Hotel, Av General de Gaulle, Raouche, T01-785300. Well-equipped dive centre offering a range of courses as well as one-time dives.
National Institute for Scuba Diving (NISD), Beirut Marina, T01-204422, www.nisd-online.com. Excellent and highly reputable dive centre that's been operating for 31 years. Offers a full range of recreational and technical dives as well as dive instructor training, and also boat charter.

Spas and beauty
You really can't pretend to be a Beiruti unless you're properly primped and preened, and you won't have any problems finding a place to pluck those eyebrows or buff those nails.
Jessy's, off Rue Nehme Yafet, Hamra. A small, unpretentious joint offering a full range of beauty treatments at extremely reasonable prices. Recommended.
Naiiman, Rue Verdun, T01-787858, www.naiiman.com. Trendy nail and hair salon with a popular male barbershop on site as well.
Salon Younes Eid, 1st floor, Starco Building, Downtown (BCD). Totally luxurious and exclusive, this high-class hair and beauty salon is frequented by Beirut's glitterati who come here for their pampering. Offers a full range of beauty services.

Sports
Beirut By Bike, Rue Al Mreisse, Ain Mreisse, T03-435524, www.beirutbybike.com. For those brave enough to take Beirut's traffic on, Beirut By Bike rent out cycles by the day.
Cyclosport, Rue Gouraud, Gemmayze, T01-446792. Daily 1030-2100. This cycle shop

rents out bikes by the hour (5000 LBP) or on a 24-hr (25,000 LBP) basis. They also sell bikes and are a great point of call if you need your own fixed.
Golf Club of Lebanon, between Blvd Ouzai and New Airport Highway, Bourj Brajneh, T01-826335, www.golfclub.org.lb, daily 0730-1930. An 18-hole course that's been keeping Beirut's golfers happy since 1923. Excellent facilities: gym, swimming pool, tennis and squash courts, pub and restaurant. Golf equipment for rent.
Hash House Harriers, http://www.geocities.com/beiruttarboush/. The Beirut chapter of the famous 'drinking club with a running problem' hosts regular runs (and walks) every 2nd Sun afternoon, and every full moon night, throughout the year. They also sometimes organize other events.
Hippodrome, near the National Museum, T01-632515, www.beiruthorseracing.com. For those who like to take a punt, the Hippodrome hosts horse racing once a week throughout the year with the day's racing taking place every Sun right through Sep-Jun (starting 1230) and on Sat during Jul-Aug (starting 1330). There are 8 races throughout the day with 10-12 horses taking part in every race.

Tour operators
For further information on recommended Beirut-based companies.

⊖ Transport

Beirut *p21, maps p30, p33 and p37*
Air
Rafiq Hariri International Airport, T01-628 195, www.beirutairport.gov.lb, is around 10 km to the south of the city centre. By far the easiest way to get to the airport is by taxi, and the going rate for tourists is US$20 (though you will hear of supreme bargainers getting the cost down to as little as US$10). If you don't feel like haggling, the simplest way is to book a taxi beforehand. To get to the airport on a budget, catch the

LCC No 1 bus, which begins in Hamra on Rue Sadat, or LCC No 5 bus, which begins in East Beirut on Ave General de Gaulle (45 mins, 1000 LBP). Both pass by at the roundabout 1 km away from the airport complex, so if you've got lots of luggage you're better off taking a taxi.

Rafiq Hariri is the main hub for Middle East Airlines (MEA), T01-622000, www.mea.com.lb, which also has an office in the Gefinor Centre in Hamra, T01-622225. MEA operate daily flights to Amman, Amsterdam, Athens, Barcelona, Cairo, Chicago, Copenhagen, Dubai, Frankfurt, Geneva, Istanbul, London, Los Angeles, Madrid, Montreal, New York, Paris, Rome and Toronto, among others. Flights to North America have a stopover in either Paris or London.

Other airlines that fly out of Beirut include Air France (T01-977977, www.airfrance.fr), BMI (T01-747777, www.flybmi.com), Egypt Air (T01-629356, www.egyptair.com), Emirates (T01-734500, www.emirates.com), Etihad (T01-975000, www.etihadairways.com), Gulf Air (T01-323332, www.gulfair.com), Lufthansa (T01-347005, www.lufthansa.com), Malaysia Airlines (T01-741344, www.malaysiaairlines.com), Pegasus Airlines (www.flypgs.com), Royal Jordanian (T01-379990, www.rj.com) and Turkish Airlines (T01-999849, www.turkishairlines.com). Departure tax is usually included in your flight ticket.

Bus

Local Although the local bus system can be tricky, there are some bus routes that are useful for visitors. The local Lebanese Commuting Company (LCC) buses are red and white and display their route number prominently on the front windscreen. Ticket prices are always either 1000 LBP or 1500 LBP. You can hail them down and get off them anywhere along the route. If you have no idea when to get off, just tell the driver your destination and he'll let you know. Some handy bus routes are listed below:
LCC Bus No 1 Hamra to Khalde: Begins in Hamra on Rue Sadat, passing Rue Verdun,

Cola Junction, the airport and Kafaat before finishing in Khalde.
LCC Bus No 2 Hamra to Antelias: Begins in Hamra on Rue Emile Edde, passing Sassine Sq in Achrafieh, Mar Mikhael, Bourj Hammoud and Dora Junction before finishing in Antelias.
LCC Bus No 5 Manara to Hay as-Saloum: Begins in Manara on Av General De Gaulle pasing Verdun and the international airport before finishing in Hay as-Saloum.
LCC Bus No 6 Cola Junction to Byblos: Begins at Cola Junction before passing through Dora Junction, Antelias, Kaslik and Jounieh before finishing in Byblos. This bus heads straight down the Antelias highway so it's your best bet for travelling to the Cilicia Museum on a budget.
LCC Bus No 8 Hamra to Ain Saadeh: Begins on Rue Sidani in Hamra and passes Sassine Sq in Achrafieh and Bourj Hammoud before finishing in Ain Saadeh. It'll get you to the Armenian district of Bourj Hammoud.

Long distance There are 2 main bus stations in Beirut. Charles Helou bus station, underneath an elevated section of Av Charles Helou, just to the east of the port area, deals with transport heading north and also transport heading to Syria, while Cola Junction bus station isn't really a bus station at all and is just a transport hub spread around a large, chaotic roundabout underneath a flyover to the southwest of the centre. It deals with all transport heading south and to the Bekaa Valley.

Charles Helou bus station is divided into sections. Zone B is for buses to Tripoli (1½ hrs). There are 2 companies operating comfortable a/c buses from here. Connexion run buses every 15 mins between 0730-1900 (4000 LBP). Tripoli Express buses are slightly older and leave every 30 mins or so (3000 LBP). You can jump off the bus at any point along the northern highway, but you'll be charged the full price to Tripoli. There are also plenty of minibuses heading north to Tripoli that congregate at the eastern side of the station (nearer Zone A). If you're heading to **Byblos**, **Batroun** or another town on the way to Tripoli this is a slightly cheaper option than the buses (usually 2000 LBP).

Zone A is for **international departures**. From here there are copious amounts of **service taxis** heading to **Damascus** (3 hrs, 800 SYP). They always quote in SYP and prefer to be paid in that currency, though you can usually convince them to accept LBP. The plus point of taking a service taxi is they leave throughout the day (you just have to wait for the taxi to fill up) and they are slightly faster than the buses. The minus point is that they are nearly always driven by seemingly suicidal maniacs.

This is also where you can catch large **luxury coaches** to Syria. There are loads of different companies to choose from but it's best to book your seat the day before travelling. **Guney Bus** has several departures daily to **Damascus** with VIP services leaving at 0530 and 0830 (3-4 hrs, 20,000 LBP) and regular services at 0930, 1030, 1230, 1800 and 2200 (3-4 hrs, 15,000 LBP). To **Aleppo**, via **Homs** and **Hama**, there are VIP services at 1030, 1400, 1515, 2230 and 2400 (5-6 hrs, 25,000 LBP) and regular services at 0830, 0930, 1230, 1630, 1900 and 2030 (5-6 hrs, 20,000 LBP).

Guney Bus also run buses to **Antakya** in Turkey with a daily departure at 2130 (8 hrs, 50,000 LBP).

Cola Junction bus station has a mixture of buses, minibuses and service taxis operating from it, primarily to destinations to the south of Beirut but also to the Bekaa Valley. From the west side of the roundabout there are regular **minibuses** to **Sidon** (1 hr, 2000 LBP) and **Chtaura** (1 hr, 4000 LBP). The buses to Chtaura often carry on to **Zahle** (1¼ hrs, 5000 LBP) and then **Baalbek** (2 hrs, 6000 LBP). If not, you can easily swap buses in Chtaura. There are also less regular minibuses to **Nabatiye** (1 hr, 5000 LBP).

This is also where you can get a **service taxi** to **Sidon** (45 mins, 5000 LBP) and **Tyre** (1½ hr, 10,000 LBP). These taxis leave quite regularly during the morning hours. Much less frequent are service taxis to **Beiteddine** (45 mins, 10,000

LBP) and to **Chtaura** (45 mins, 10,000 LBP). These only leave if enough passengers turn up so come early for your best chance.

If you can't get a service taxi to Beiteddine, a minibus to the **Chouf** leaves from just north of the main service taxi/minibus stand. Keeping the flyover on your right, cross the road from the main bus stand and walk 2 blocks up the road. The bus leaves regularly from a small unsigned parking space just after the Hafez Motors building and just before the road intersection. This bus passes by the road junction a short walk from **Beiteddine** itself (1 hr, 2500 LBP).

The eastern side of the roundabout is the starting point for the **LCC No 6 bus** to **Byblos** (1½ hrs, 1500 LBP). If you are heading anywhere along the north coast up to Byblos this bus is a great option as it takes the old coast highway so that you can be dropped inside the towns rather than on the highway.

As well as the above main 2 transport hubs, at **Dora Junction** on the Antelias highway, past Bourj Hammoud, you can pick up any of the transport heading north from Charles Helou bus station. On **Rue Badaro** just south of the National Museum ('Mathaf' in Arabic) you can catch **LCC bus No 7** to **Beit Meri** and **Broummana** in Mount Lebanon.

Car hire
Avis Airport, T01-629890; Downtown (Phoenicia Intercontinental Hotel), T01-363848; www.avis.com.lb.
Budget, Rue Madame Curie, Hamra, T01-740741; www.budget-rental.com.
Hala Rent-a-car, Airport, T01-629444; Dunes Centre, Rue Verdun, T01-793333; www.halacar.com.
Lenacar/Europcar, Airport, T01-629888; Gefinor Plaza, Hamra, T01-364656; www.lenacar.com.
Hertz, Airport, T01-628998; www.hertz.com.
Sixt Rent-a-car, Corniche el-Mazraa, T01-301226, www.sixt.com.lb.

Service taxis and private taxis
See also page 22.

Although many Beirut taxis don't have a 'taxi' sign on their roof, you can spot a service/private taxi by its number plates. All taxis must have red number plates to distinguish them from private vehicles.

Service (shared) taxis are the most popular form of local transport in Beirut. They are numerous and highly persistent, beeping and kerb crawling anyone who looks like a potential customer (which in effect means anyone on foot). Trying to cross the road can sometimes be very frustrating with service taxis constantly slowing down in front of you just when there would otherwise be a gap in the traffic. They simply head for the destination of their first passenger and then look for more customers along the way.

The standard price of a service taxi ride anywhere within the city is 2000 LBP but if the driver wasn't going that way, or thinks your destination is too far away he may say 'serveece-ain' ('double service'), which costs 4000 LBP. There is no rhyme or reason to this pricing; it's up to the discretion of the individual taxi driver. If you don't want to pay double the price, wait for the next taxi to come along; he may be happy to only charge you a single fare. Always confirm that the taxi is operating as a service taxi ('serveece') before getting in.

Getting to grips with the system takes some time. It helps to position yourself along a major road heading in the overall direction that you wish to go, bearing in mind the 1-way system. Thus, to head east from Hamra, you need to be on Rue Emile Edde/Rue Spears; service taxis running along Rue Hamra will all take you out towards Manara and Raouche.

Most of the service taxis will also operate as private taxis if you want. The standard rate for a journey inside the city is 10,000 LBP, though for some shorter trips you may only be charged 5000-6000 LBP. Always agree on a price before getting into the taxi. Late at night you can expect to pay double. If you don't want to hail a taxi on the street, most hotels can book a taxi to pick you up.

All the below taxis can be booked for half and full-day sightseeing journeys throughout the country as well as for shorter trips within the city itself: **Alfa Taxi**, T01-560910; **Allo Taxi**, T01-366661; **Charlie Taxi**, T01-265205; **Imad Maged**, T03-053713. Imad comes highly recommended by travellers for half- and full-day sightseeing journeys for his honesty, excellent driving and genuine interest in providing good service.

Directory

Beirut *p21, maps p30, p33 and p37*
Banks Banks generally open Mon-Fri 0830-1400 and Sat 0830-1200, though some of the bigger branches open to 1600 on weekdays. You'll find lots of banks with ATMs along Rue Hamra and Rue Makdissi in Hamra and there are also lots of money exchange offices in this area. Downtown, you'll find ATMs scattered around the streets leading off Place d'Etoile and banks with ATMs all along Rue Riad es-Solh, while in East Beirut there are banks with ATMs along all the main streets, including Av Charles Malik and Rue Gouraud. Money exchange offices stay open later than banks and most will change practically every imaginable currency. Rates on any currency other than US$ vary slightly, so shop around. **Lord's Exchange** on Rue Hamra is a good choice. Traveller's cheques (TCs) always attract a commission rate, and you are much better off using a combination of ATMs and cash. In an emergency, you can have money sent to you quickly through Western Union Money Transfer, although this works out very expensive. The main agents in Beirut include **Byblos Bank** and **Lebanese Canadian Bank**.
Cultural centres The foreign cultural centres in Beirut are primarily geared towards providing language courses and information on their respective countries for the Lebanese, but are also of interest to tourists for their newspapers and magazines, film nights, cultural programmes and occasional lectures. Always take your passport along if you want to access a

centre. The French centre is the most active. **British Council**, Berytech Building, Rue Damascus, T01-428900, www.britishcouncil.org/lebanon, Mon-Fri 0900-1800. Has a small library and organizes art exhibitions, film showings and theatre events. **French Cultural Centre (CCF)**, Rue Damascus (near the National Museum), T01-420230, www.ambafrance-liban.org.lb. Has a monthly program of events and art exhibitions, hosts regular film nights and boasts a large library. **Goethe Institute**, Berytech Building, Rue Damascus, T01-422291, www.goethe.de/beirut. Has a varied program of lectures, events, exhibitions and concerts as well as a good library. **Instituto Cervantes**, Rue Maarad, Downtown, T01-970253, www.cervantes.es. There is a decent library here and the centre hosts occasional exhibitions and events. **Embassies and consulates** Embassy hours are generally Mon-Fri 0800-1200 or 1500. Note that most embassies only issue visas to Lebanese nationals, so there is not much point trying to get visas for onward travel here; it's a much better idea to organize this from your home country. One exception to this is the new **Syrian Embassy** which is, at the moment, issuing tourist visas to foreign nationals. Note that some embassies are based in Mount Lebanon rather than in Beirut. To make searching for an embassy easier, the Mount Lebanon embassies have been listed below as well. **Australia**, Embassy Complex, Rue Serail, Downtown, T01-960600. **Austria**, Tabaris Building, Av Charles Malik, T01-213017. **Belgium**, Rue Emir Bashir, T01-976001. **Canada**, Coolrite Building, Jal al-Dib Highway, Mt Lebanon, T04-710591. **Denmark**, Tabaris Building, Av Charles Malik, T01-991001. **France**, Rue Damascus, (near the National Museum), T01-420000. **Germany**, near Jesus and Mary School, Mtayleb, Mt Lebanon, T04-929600. **Greece**, Antoine Abu Khater Building, Rue Embassy, Naccache, Mt Lebanon, T04-521700. **India**, Rue Kantari, T01-372619. **Iran**, Rue Shehab, Bir Hassan, T01-821224. **Iraq**, Rue Pierre

Helou, Hazmieh, Mt Lebanon, T05-459940. **Italy**, Baabda, Mt Lebanon, T05-954955. **Japan**, Embassy Complex, Rue Serail, Downtown, T01-989751. **Jordan**, Rue Elias Helou, Baabda, T05-922500. **Netherlands**, Netherlands Tower, Av Charles Malik, Ashrafieh, T01-204663. **Spain**, Antounieh, Mt Lebanon, T05-464120. **Switzerland**, Av Fouad Chehab, T01-324129. **Syria**, Rue Makdissi , Hamra, T01-735849. To apply for a tourist visa you'll need a letter of recommendation from your home country's embassy (usually easily obtainable but expensive), 2 passport photos and photocopies of your passport information page and Lebanese visa page. Take these along with your passport to the Syrian Embassy. All nationalities (except USA) can be issued with a Syrian tourist visa in 3 days. Citizens of the USA can be issued with a tourist visa here as well, but the process will take 20-25 days. All in all, it's much easier, and less expensive, to apply for your Syrian tourist visa in your home country. **Turkey**, Rabieh, Mt Lebanon, T04-520929. **UK**, Embassy Complex, Rue Serail, Downtown, T01-960800. **USA**, Rue Amin Gemayel, Aoukar, Mt Lebanon, T04-542600.

Internet Many of the hotels in Beirut have Wi-Fi but you usually have to pay for it. In contrast, nearly all of the city's cafés provide Wi-Fi access for free. Be warned though, on the whole connections are on the slow side. There are plenty of internet cafés dotted around the city. Most charge 3000 LBP per hr. **Net Café**, just off Rue Makdissi (on Rue Antoun Gemayel) is a friendly place with a super-fast connection most of the time. On Rue Sidani there are a couple of good places: both **Net Café** and **Virus** have a decent amount of terminals, though Virus tends to be busy with kids playing computer games.

Language courses Centre for Arab and Middle Eastern Studies (CAMES), American University of Beirut, T01-350000, www.aub.edu.lb. Every summer CAMES runs an extremely well-regarded, 8-week, intensive Arabic language program with 7 levels of study to choose from. It's a demanding course and not cheap (course fees are US$4050), but if you're serious about studying Arabic this is an excellent option. Classes generally run Mon-Fri for 6 hrs per day. Applications to enrol in the course must be made by Mar and details can be found on their website. **Saifi Institute**, Rue Pasteur, Gemmayze, T01-560738, www.saifiarabic. com. This private language centre runs a range of courses throughout the year specializing in teaching practical day-to-day Arabic skills. Course levels cater for the complete novice to the advanced speaker and cost between US$240-600 dependent on how intensive your course is. Accommodation is available for students at Saifi Urban Gardens, which is based in the same building and run by the same people. Highly recommended by expats living in Beirut. **Talk Beirut**, T03-436261, www. bebeirut.org/talk. If you want to hit the ground running with your language skills, the 5-hr crash course Talk Beirut offers could be for you. Classes (costing 100,000 LBP for the course, which is usually split into 2 sessions) take place in the Hamra area and cover basic conversation skills, all using the Lebanese dialect, and catered to your particular language needs. You can also sign up for longer-term private lessons costing 22,000 LBP per hr. **Laundry** Most of the laundries in Beirut are dry cleaners, which works out very expensive if you need to get a lot washed. In Hamra, on Rue Sidani, **Laundromatic** is a coin-operated laundry with a big load costing around 4500 LBP. All the hotels in Beirut offer a laundry service. In the budget places this can be very good value (you may even simply be allowed to use the washing machine for a small fee, or for free). In the more expensive hotels everything will be painstakingly dry-cleaned, ironed and folded (and probably individually wrapped in plastic), but you will pay through the nose for the service. **Medical services** There are numerous private hospitals dotted around Beirut. The

American University Hospital (AUH), Rue Omar Ben Abdul Aziz, Hamra, T01-350000, is centrally located and has excellent facilities as well as a well stocked pharmacy. There are dozens of good pharmacies throughout the city. **Post office** The central post office is on Rue Riad es-Solh, Downtown. In Hamra there is a post office on Rue Makdissi, across the road and a few doors down from the Embassy Hotel. In East Beirut there is a post office on Rue Gouraud in Gemmayze and another on Sassine Sq in Achrafieh.

Telephone There are numerous card-phones scattered throughout Beirut. The hard part is finding one in a quiet location. The ones in Downtown, in the streets off Place d'Etoile are probably your best bet, as this area is closed off to traffic. Most internet cafés have Skype services uploaded on their computers.

Visa extensions To extend your 1-month tourist visa, at least a couple of days before your visa expires you need to head to the **Directorate Securite Generale**, on Rue Damascus, across the road from the National Museum. Take your passport, 2 passport photos and 2 photocopies of your passport information page and Lebanese visa page. Visa extensions are handled on the 2nd floor. Come early as it can get very busy by about 1000, and you may have to queue for up to 1 hr. Once processed, you'll be issued with a receipt and told to come and collect your passport in 7 days' time. To collect your passport, bring your receipt with you and, instead of going inside the main building, take the path to the right of the main entrance that leads around to the back of the building. There is a window here where you queue to hand in your receipt and receive your passport back. You will be issued with a free visa that extends your tourist visa for another 2 months. This is the extension limit on tourism visas. If you want to stay longer you will have to leave the country and come back on a new visa.

Contents

Footprint features

Mount Lebanon

Background

It's important to distinguish Mount Lebanon from the Lebanon mountain range, the latter consisting of the entire coastal range running the whole length of the country. Arab geographers used the term Mount Lebanon rather loosely, to refer to the higher northern parts of the Lebanon mountains, between Tripoli and Byblos, and this appears to be the perception of Crusader chroniclers.

During the 17th century the Druze emir **Fakhr ud-Din II Maan**, who had his base in the Chouf Mountains, was appointed by the **Ottomans** to administer what were then the Sanjaks of Beirut and Sidon (essentially the Chouf and Kesrouan). He briefly managed to extend his control northwards also, to include Mount Lebanon, before being deposed by the Ottomans who feared that he had become too powerful.

By the early 19th century the **Emir Bashir Shihab II** had once again succeeded in uniting all the mountain districts – from Mount Lebanon in the north to the Chouf Mountains in the south – under his control, this time more permanently, and the whole of this mountainous area became known as Mount Lebanon. After 1860, when the Ottomans were forced, under pressure from the European powers, to create the special semi-autonomous *Mutasarrifiya* of Mount Lebanon, it was defined as including all of this area and for the first time, officially at least, Mount Lebanon became a political entity.

The motivation behind the creation of this entity was to protect the Maronite Christians, who formed a majority within it, but who had suffered terrible massacres at the hands of the Druze in 1860. The presence of significant numbers of Maronites in the Chouf Mountains dates back to the 17th century when Emir Fakhr ud-Din II Maan began encouraging them to settle in these areas to help with the labour-intensive production of silk, which soon became a flourishing and highly lucrative industry. Earlier, in the 16th century, the Maronites had begun the process of southward migration, settling in the Kesrouan at the invitation of the Assaf clan. This process continued through the 18th and early 19th centuries under the Shihab emirs, to the extent that Maronites came to be responsible for most of the silk production, although the land they worked was mostly rented from Druze landowners.

When the Ottomans imposed their direct rule over the former territories of Emir Bashir Shihab II in 1840, they divided that territory into two administrative regions, and began playing off the Maronites and Druze against each other in an attempt to subdue them both. It was to a large extent this policy of divide and rule that led to the massacres of 1860.

The civil war of 1975-1990 saw what was in many ways a repeat of these events in the coastal mountains, with the Druze establishing their supremacy in the Chouf Mountains, while the Kesrouan region provided the main heartland of support for the Maronite Phalange militia of the Gemayel family. The Metn, meanwhile, and the Beirut–Damascus highway in particular, became the front line between the Maronites and Druze.

The Metn

Directly east of Beirut, the mountains of the Metn rise steeply from the coastal plain. A number of summer resorts have grown up in these mountains – places where Beirutis can come to escape the heat and humidity of the city. The most popular are Beit Meri and Broummana, which can both be visited as a short round trip from Beirut, returning via the town of Bikfaya on the alternative route between Beirut and Zahle. While the views may be impressive and the summer climate appealing, the popularity of this region and its proximity to Beirut have also in a sense been its undoing, with an often ugly sprawl of development spreading up the mountains along the roads leading out of Beirut. ➼ *For listings, see pages 62-65.*

Beit Meri and Broummana

At an altitude of 770-800 m above sea level, both Beit Meri and Broummana are refreshingly cool in summer and offer spectacular views out over Beirut and the Mediterranean. Beit Meri, where the archaeological site of Deir el-Qalaa is located, has grown to a considerable size in recent years, with numerous private villas and apartments belonging to rich Beirutis spread across the hillside. There are a couple of hotels here, and on the road between Beit Meri and Broummana, but it is Broummana itself that is the prime summer resort.

Broummana is spread out for several kilometres along the main road, with another road running parallel to the southeast. There is nothing of special interest as such here, this being more a place to come and enjoy the views and lively atmosphere in summer, dine out in style and indulge in a bit of nightlife.

Getting there and away

If you're coming by public transport, LCC bus No 7 leaves about every 20 minutes from near the National Museum in Beirut and travels through Beit Meri, Broummana and onto Bikfaya.

If you're driving from Beirut it can be a little tricky to navigate your way out of the city to pick up the road to Beit Meri. Head southeast from Downtown on Rue de Damas. Turn left at the National Museum junction and then after around 500 m turn right at the large intersection and flyover to join the broad dual carriageway of Ave Elias Hrawi (signposted for Chtaura). Follow signs for Sin el-Fil (this involves looping underneath Ave Elias Hrawi by the glass Cellis building), and then for Mkalles. Arriving at a large roundabout ('Place Sin el-Fil'), turn right. At the next roundabout ('Place Mkalles'), go straight across, this being the start of the road up to Beit Meri and Broummana (signposted 'Route de Baabdat').

The road climbs steeply into the mountains through a more or less continuous sprawl of suburbs. Some 2 km from the Mkalles roundabout the road forks; left is signposted for

Beit Meri, though in fact both branches join up again before Beit Meri. Going by either route, a little over 9 km from the Mkalles roundabout, soon after a sign announcing the start of Beit Meri, you can either follow the road sharply round to the left to continue on to Broummana, or bear off to the right to visit Deir el-Qalaa (see below; signposted 'Ruines de Beit-Mery' on a Ministry of Tourism signboard). Following the road sharply round to the left, after just over 1 km bear left at a roundabout with a column in the centre. A little under 2 km further on, you have the option of forking left (signposted 'Centre Ville') by the massive new **Grand Hills** resort, or else carrying straight on. Both roads take you through Broummana before joining up again at the western end of town; the left fork is the more interesting route through town and gives the best views. ▸▸ *See Transport, page 65.*

Deir el-Qalaa

ⓘ *Daily sunrise-sunset, free. To reach the site, bear right at the junction soon after the start of Beit Meri (coming from Beirut; see route description, above), and then bear right again at a mini roundabout 400 m further on. After a further 400 m or so, a track off to the left (with a large Ministry of Tourism sign beside it) leads up to the site.*

Deir el-Qalaa consists of a 17th-century Maronite monastery standing on the ruins of a Roman temple, with further Roman and Byzantine ruins nearby. The most interesting sight here is the beautiful piece of mosaic flooring hidden away amid the tumble of weeds in the Roman/Byzantine ruin area. If you are staying in Beit Meri or nearby Broummana, or have come here for the day to escape the city heat below, this site is well worth visiting.

Inscriptions discovered here by Julius Löytved (the vice-consul of Denmark during the late 19th century and a keen amateur archaeologist) have identified the Roman temple as being dedicated to *Baal Marcod* (the 'Lord of Dances'), and there is evidence to suggest that this was built on the site of an earlier Phoenician temple.

The **Maronite monastery**, built of stones from the Roman temple, was heavily damaged during the civil war, but since then has been extensively restored. A number of hefty columns can be seen, including one built into the wall of the monastery, and also a large square platform built of massive stone blocks, possibly the base of the *cella* of the Roman temple. Nearby there are the remains of other smaller temples, including one dedicated to the goddess Juno, dating from the reign of Trajan (AD 98-117).

Heading back down the road, on both sides, there is an extensive area of **Roman and Byzantine** ruins mostly consisting of fallen columns and capitals amidst overgrown scrub and unfortunately strewn with rubbish. Although these ruins may look unsubstantial at first, on the right-hand side of the road is a very impressive area of **mosaic flooring** that was part of a sixth-century Byzantine church and also the remains of a baths complex. Both are behind the first house you come to.

A driving route through the Metn to Zahle

As well as offering a much quieter and more scenic route to Zahle compared with the main Beirut–Damascus highway, this road gives you excellent views of Jebel Sannine. Note that beyond Mrouj, the road is blocked by snow during the winter; if you wish to attempt it in early spring or late autumn, check first that it is open. A lengthy diversion off this route brings you to the small ski resort of **Qanat Bakich**, from where you can also continue on to **Faqra**. En route to Qanat Bakich you pass through the village of **Baskinta**, from where a narrow mountain road loops around the lower slopes of Jebel Sannine to rejoin the Bikfaya–Zahle road between Majdel Tarchich and Zahle.

Beirut to Bikfaya

From Beirut, join the coastal motorway heading north and take the Antelias exit. The road climbs steadily through a more or less continuous built-up sprawl to arrive at Bikfaya (14 km from the motorway exit), the start of which is marked by a roundabout with a large modernistic monument in the centre. Bearing sharp right here (signposted to Baabdat and Broummana, amongst others) puts you on the road to **Broummana** and Beit Meri (see page 124). Continuing straight on into the centre of town, bear right after 600 m to pick up the road for **Dhour ech-Choueir** (signposted) and **Zahle** (going straight leads you into a confusing though very scenic maze of tiny mountain roads).

You can continue northeast from Broummana along a picturesque road leading to Bikfaya. After passing through the village of Baabdat, there is a viewpoint offering excellent views of Jebel Knisseh to the right (east). Soon after, go straight across a roundabout (right for Douar) and then through a couple more villages to arrive at a roundabout at the eastern end of **Bikfaya**, 11 km from Broummana. Turn sharp left here to head back down to Beirut, joining the coastal motorway at Antelias.

Bikfaya

Bikfaya has a certain air of prosperity about it. This is the home town of the Gemayel family; Pierre Gemayel, founder of the Phalange party in 1936; Bashir Gemayel, the leader of the Phalange militia and Lebanese president-elect for less than a month before his murder in 1982; and Amin Gemayel, Lebanese president from 1982-1988. Their presence is strongly stamped on the town, most notably in the family's 'Presidence', a beautiful Ottoman period mansion signposted off to the left (north) of the main road (though strictly off-limits unless you have some pretty good connections). Bikfaya suffered heavily during 1987 when fighting broke out between the Phalange and various other Christian militias for control of the area. However, the wealth and influence of the Gemayel family ensured that it was rapidly rebuilt. During August of each year a **flower festival** is held here. There are several restaurants and a number of hotels, but otherwise the town has little to offer of special interest.

Getting there and away During summer, service taxis run from Dora Junction in Beirut to Bikfaya and there are minibuses from here as well. Services are much less frequent in winter.

Bikfaya to Baskinta and Qanat Bakich

Heading out of Bikfaya on the road towards Dhour ech-Choueir, you pass first through the village of **Douar**, where the damage caused by the internecine fighting between Christian militias in 1987 can still be seen.

Continue straight through the village, passing a right turn leading towards Broummana and Beit Meri, to arrive in **Dhour ech-Choueir**, 5 km from Bikfaya. Travelling in this direction, the main road bypasses the centre of the village; turn left to reach the centre, where there is the imposing Maronite St Mary's church. Continuing along the main road, you pass through a beautiful area of pine forest known as **Bois de Boulogne** (marked on most maps as **Bolonia**), arriving after 7 km at a crossroads and checkpoint. To make the diversion to **Baskinta** and **Qanat Bakich**, turn left at the crossroads.

Heading towards Qanat Bakich, the road descends to the village of **Bteghrine** (follow signs for Baskinta and Qanat Bakich). You may have to ask directions through the village as the route through it is rather confusing. From here the road winds its way steeply down into the deep Wadi el-Jamajin and up the other side to arrive in **Baskinta** (15 km from the crossroads). Turn sharp left in the village (signposted in Arabic only, so ask directions), and then bear right at a fork 1 km further on (signposted to Qanat Bakich, and also to Faqra and Faraya). The road climbs steadily for a further 7 km to arrive in **Qanat Bakich**.

Baskinta

The picturesque town of Baskinta, with its abundance of traditional red-roofed buildings so typical of this region, is interesting for its many literary connections. This was the home town of the poet Mikhail Neameh who, along with Khalil Gibran, was a founding member of the New York literary society The Pen League, and his tomb and family's summer house can be seen in the village. These are just two sites that form part of the larger **Baskinta Literary Trail** (BLT); a 24-km walking route that begins here.

The BLT passes 22 literary landmarks in the countryside around Baskinta, showcasing this area's importance in Lebanon's artistic heritage. As well as Mikhail Neaimeh, this town and the surrounding area has also played host to, among others, the poet and journalist Abdullah Ghanem and the artist Georges Aroyan. Nearby in Ain el Qabou, which the BLT passes through, is the summer home of Amin Maalouf, one of Lebanon's most internationally famous writers, who currently resides in France.

There is an excellent accommodation option within Baskinta itself, making it a great place to spend a couple of days walking in the surrounding countryside and enjoying the quiet pace of life.

Metn & Kesrouan

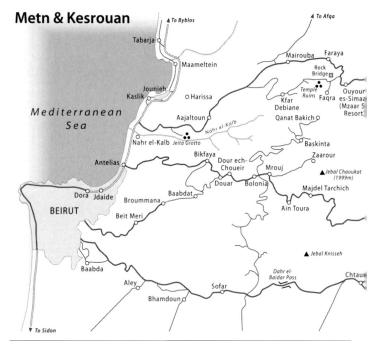

Qanat Bakich ski resort

ⓘ *Mon-Fri 0800-1530, Sat-Sun/public holidays 0800-1600, US$10 weekdays, US$18 weekends.*
First established in 1967 by the Karam family who built the first ski lift here, Qanat Bakich suffered considerable damage during the civil war and had to be completely redeveloped afterwards. This resort, popular in the early 1970s for its good snow and interesting slopes, is Lebanon's smallest and its non-crowded slopes are a definite bonus. It's an excellent choice for less experienced skiers, with four out of their five slopes suitable for beginners. Ski and snowboard equipment can be hired from the **Snowland Hotel** (the resort's one accommodation option) or from one of the rental shops nearby. Full equipment hire generally costs US$5-12. Those wanting to stay overnight are not limited to the Snowland, as the accommodation at nearby Faraya village is only a 10-minute drive away.

Qanat Bakich to Faqra

From the Snowland Hotel, bear right for the ski lift; if you bear left it is a further 4 km on to the private **Faqra Ski Club** (see page 69). On a clear day, you can see spectacular views down the Wadi Daraiya and Nahr el-Kalb Valley to the Mediterranean. When arriving in Faqra Ski Club you'll see a barrier across the road, but the attendant seems happy to let people through. You can then continue on to Faraya/Mzaar and/or head back down to the coast via Aajaltoun.

Baskinta to Zahle

To carry on to Zahle you can either head back to the crossroads and checkpoint or continue straight using the following directions.

From the crossroads and checkpoint, 1 km further on you arrive at a roundabout and church in the centre of **Mrouj**. Turn right here for Zahle (or straight on – keeping the church to your left – to reach the private, members-only skiing club of **Zaarour**, 7 km away). Taking the Zahle road, after 5 km you pass through **Ain Toura**, a small, rather ugly village consisting mostly of new concrete buildings. The road then begins to climb steeply into the beautiful and rugged limestone mountains of Jebel ech-Chaoukat/Jebel Knisseh. At **Majdel Tarchich** (9 km from Mrouj) there are a couple of snack places. The road continues to climb through a surreal landscape of weathered limestone rock before reaching the crest of the mountains, from where there are stunning views down into the Bekaa Valley, with the Anti-Lebanon Mountains beyond. From here the road descends steadily down to Zahle, 31 km from Mrouj.

Alternatively, if you continue straight on through the village of Baskinta (not taking the sharp left to head up to Qanat Bakich),

you can rejoin the Bikfaya–Zahle road roughly halfway between Majdel Tarchich and Zahle. This narrow and extremely beautiful mountain road works its way around the head of the green and wooded Jamajin Valley, with the bare, imposing southwest slopes of Jebel Sannine rising majestically above.

After around 8 km you pass through the village of **Sannine**, where there are several restaurants all with stunning views down the valley. From here, the road climbs up over the lower slopes of Jebel Sannine, passing a couple of small, high-altitude lakes before descending and arriving at the Bikfaya–Zahle road (19 km from Baskinta). Turning left, it is around 11 km down to Zahle, or turning right, around 20 km to Mrouj.

The Metn listings

For Sleeping and Eating price codes and other relevant information, see pages 9-10.

 Sleeping

Beit Meri and Broummana *p57*

Not a place for budget travellers, during summer Beit Meri and Broummana attract their fair share of Gulf and local tourists who retreat here for a cool respite from the coast. Many rent apartments for the entire summer and the hotels here tend to be on the expensive side, so if you're in that price bracket and not a city person, both Beit Meri and Broummana are good alternatives to staying in Beirut.

Price categories quoted here are for the high season, when advance booking is recommended. During the low season most hotels offer substantial discounts (as much as 50% in some cases). Many of the luxury hotels also run promotions throughout the year with their rack rates considerably reduced, so it's worthwhile checking their websites for deals.

Traditionally, the high season lasts from the beginning of May or Jun through to the end of Nov or Dec, though in practice it is much shorter these days, really only lasting from mid-Jul through to mid-Sep. All the hotels listed below stay open year round.

$$$$ Al Bustan, Beit Meri (signposted from all directions), T04-972980, www. albustanhotel.com. A wonderful alternative to the international chain hotels of Beirut, the Al Bustan is a family-owned, independent hotel that sits high and mighty over the village of Beit Meri. The surrounding views of the countryside are superb, and the hotel supports the arts (it hosts an annual festival and has its own art collection on display throughout the hotel). Rooms are definitely comfortable (as you'd expect at this price) with the latest technology installed, a/c, minibar and excellent beds as standard, but it's still a tad expensive for what you get. Swimming pool, several bars and restaurants, excellent conference facilities, free airport pickup, breakfast included.

$$$$ Grand Hills, Rue Al Charkiah, Broummana, T04-868888, www. grandhillsvillage.com. If you're after all-encompassing resort swish, Grand Hills has it in spades. This massive complex is a luxurious hideaway from the rest of the world with 3 swimming pools, its own spa, gym, multiple restaurants and bars, a shopping arcade and huge gardens. The rooms here have all the mod cons you'd expect and have been decorated according to 'theme'. The result, on the whole, is that they are elegant and individually quirky, but it must be said that some of the room 'themes' do verge on the tacky.

$$$ Le Crillon, Broummana centre, T04-865555, www.lecrillon.com. Welcoming and family-run, the rooms here (a/c, satellite TV, minibar and balcony) are decent-sized, clean and bright, though they are more business-style rather than a holiday hotel. Restaurant, bar, swimming pool, gym.

$$$ Printania Palace, Rue Chahine Achkar, Broummana, T04-862000, www. printania.com. The tasteful, though slightly bland, rooms (a/c, satellite TV, balcony and minibar) here are set back from the road and surrounded by gardens, making this a quiet retreat. With resort-like facilities (restaurants, swimming pool, large grounds with children's play area), it's quite good value compared with some of the other hotels in the area, though asking an extra US$18 for breakfast is a bit steep.

$$ Garden, Broummana centre, T04-960579, This friendly family hotel has decent-sized rooms (a/c, satellite TV) that all come with balcony, and there's a swimming pool and restaurant too. Outside of peak season the discounts you can get are brilliant value.

$$ Kanaan, Broummana centre, T04-960084. A good value and decent place right across the road from Broummana high school. Cheerful basic rooms all come with bathrooms that could do with an update but at this price, in this town, you can't complain. Grab a room with a balcony if you can. Outside of peak season the rooms are even cheaper.

$$ Pax, Broummana centre, T04-960027. A welcoming place with a peculiar pink colour scheme that thankfully doesn't follow you into the rooms. The rooms could do with a refurb and the bathrooms are a tad on the small side, but they're clean and all come with a/c, satellite TV, fridge and balcony. The large sun terrace on the roof with its hilarious lurid green fake-grass carpet is an added bonus.

Bikfaya to Baskinta and Qanat Bakich *p59*
$$ Grand Hotel Bois de Boulogne, on the right immediately before the check-post and crossroads, Bois de Boulogne, T04-295100. This grand old dame of a hotel is a lovely old-fashioned place that evokes an atmosphere of yesteryear. Pleasant rooms (a/c, satellite TV, Wi-Fi and balcony) are clean

and decently sized and there are also larger bungalows nestled between the leafy trees in the large garden out back.

Baskinta *p60*
$$ Khoury Hanna Guesthouse, T04-250084. This delightful family guesthouse is set in one of Baskinta's traditional stone-walled and red-tiled houses, with much of its original interior features preserved. The simple and super-clean rooms here, along with the delicious food and the welcoming hosts, make it a great place to stop for the night if you're exploring the area. Member of the DHIAFEE hotel network.

Qanat Bakich ski resort *p61*
$$ Snowland, T03-340300 (or Beirut T01-870077), www.snowland.com.lb. Qanat Bakich's only hotel, the Snowland is right on the slopes and has good-value rooms that are simple but comfortable (satellite TV, heater, some with balcony) and helpful staff. There are great facilities here for the price, with a heated indoor swimming pool, restaurant serving decently priced meals and all the amenities you need for a ski holiday: ski hire, ski school, a first-aid team based at the hotel on weekends and ski lifts right outside. It's an excellent family choice.

🍴 Eating

Beit Meri and Broummana *p57*
These summer retreats are all about the food. Boasting some excellent fine dining options, places here tend to be on the pricey side and are patronized by a 'see-and-be-seen' crowd. If you're on a budget there's a few less expensive options strung out on Broummana's main road, but nothing of particular note. There are also 2 excellent supermarkets to stock up on essentials. Both **Bechara** and **Ara** supermarket are on the main road, next door to each other.

♟♟♟ Burj al-Hamam, around 1 km out of Broummana, heading towards Baabdat and Bikfaya (signposted off to the right of the road), T04-960058. Daily 1200-late. This huge and upmarket restaurant provides something of a spectacle in summer, when the seriously rich come here in their droves to dine. All your favourite meze and grills feature on the menu, which focuses on finely done Lebanese staples. Dress smart and arrive in a flash car or you may not be made to feel overly welcome.

₮₮₮ Il Giadino, Al Bustan hotel, Beit Meri. This long-standing Italian restaurant is your best bet in town if you're feeling like a plate of pasta. The tasty dishes here may be expensive but they're well executed and definitely worth it.

₮₮₮ Le Gargotier, Broummana centre, T04-960562. Tue-Sun 1200-1500, 1900-2400. First established in 1971, this cosy traditional French restaurant is an intimate and stylish dining option that's perfect for a romantic dinner for 2.

₮₮₮ Mounir, off main road between Beit Meri and Broummana (coming from Broummana, just after you pass the **Bellevue Palace Hotel**, a signposted fork off to the right leads down steeply to the restaurant), T04-873900. Daily 1200-late. The foodie's choice, Mounir is famous for its perfectly executed Levantine cuisine. A wonderful place for a late, long and lazy lunch, this large and very classy upmarket Lebanese restaurant has extensive gardens and a terrace. If you're travelling with kids, they'll be kept happy with a children's play area on site. It's pricey, but the food really is excellent.

₮₮ Kings, Broummana centre. Popular American-diner style place with comfy booth-type seating. There's a large menu of burgers and other fast-food style favourites.

₮ Café Kanaan, Broummana centre. The friendly atmosphere here makes it a continually popular spot. This place is excellent value, with a delicious menu of pizzas, burgers and crêpes all under 10,000 LBP. It hovers undecidedly between a bar and a café/restaurant, so it's as good for a lunchtime snack on the terrace as it is for a few beers in the evening.

⊙ Entertainment

Beit Meri and Broummana *p57*
As a popular summer getaway from Beirut, Broummana has plenty of bars to service the party crowd. Late in the evening it can get pretty hectic and crowded.

Cheers, Broummana centre. A no-nonsense bar set inside a lovely vaulted room that can get packed out on Fri and Sat nights in the height of summer. The service is great and the crowd is friendly, but don't come here for a quiet drink because this place does loud like it's going out of fashion.

Oaks Pub, Broummana centre. A lovely relaxed place to come for a few drinks. Slightly more refined than the other choices in town.

Taboo Pub, Broummana centre. Although it was pumping out some pretty tacky music when we visited, it's forgiven for its quick, friendly service and good-time crowd.

⊙ Festivals and events

Beit Meri and Broummana *p57*
Feb-Mar Al Bustan Festival, www.albustanfestival.com. See page 28.

▲ Activities and tours

Baskinta *p60*
As one of the villages along the Lebanon Mountain Trail (and also having its own literary-based hiking trail) Baskinta is a great base for hiking and trekking in the region. Some good, local hiking guides are:
Carlos Hobeika, T03-580901.
Carole Akl, T03-825064.
George Hobeika, T03-451113.

⊖ Transport

Beit Meri and Broummana *p57*
Both the red and white **LCC No 7** bus and
the blue and white **OFTC No 17** bus wind
their way up and down the main roads of
Beit Meri and Broummana throughout the
day. The OFTC bus heads as far as **Bikfaya**,
while the LCC bus doubles back a couple
of kilometres short of Bikfaya. You can flag
them down anywhere along the route. The
LCC bus has the most frequent services,
with a bus usually every 20 mins or so
throughout the day. Heading back to **Beirut**
(45 mins), both buses terminate just to the
southeast of the National Museum. Journeys
on this route are a flat fee of 1000 LBP.

If you get stuck with no transport back to
Beirut the **Achkar taxi office** (T04-961041) is
on Broummana's main road.

ⓘ Directory

Beit Meri and Broummana *p57*
Banks Broummana's banks all have
ATMs and are spread out along the main
road. They include **Bank Med**, **SGBL Bank**
and **Credit Libanais**. There is an efficient
money exchange opposite Bank Med.
Internet Internet cafés have a tendency
to come and go here quite regularly. On
Broummana's main road **Touti Net** is quite
well established. **Laundry** Right beside Café
Kanaan, **Clean Xpress** has fast and efficient
service. **Medical services** Just opposite
Bank Med, **Pharmacy Joe** is well stocked and
has English-speaking staff. **Post office** Both
Broummana and Beit Meri have post offices.
Beit Meri's is on the main road through town
while Broummana's is just off the main road.

The Kesrouan

A winter-sports enthusiast's dream, the Kesrouan mountain region is home to the ski slopes of Jebel Sannine (2628 m). During the season the road up here is bumper-to-bumper traffic as keen skiers and snowboarders head up to Lebanon's most popular ski resort, Mzaar. Most of the winter action revolves around the twin mountain villages of Faraya and Ouyoun es-Simaan, a hop-skip-and-jump to the slopes, although those with the right contacts might be able to wrangle an invite to ski at the nearby private ski club of Faqra.

Backed by the dramatic eroded limestone formations of the mountains, this area is a hive of activity during the season. When the snow disappears, both Faraya and Ouyoun es-Simaan press the snooze button and revert back to charmingly sleepy alpine hamlets. If you're road-tripping through the country during this time, the interesting Faqra ruins nearby are worth a stop, while the main Kesrouan access road is the starting point for some excellent day-long drives. Just before Faraya you can divert off the main road to approach the Adonis Valley from the southwest; a beautifully scenic drive along a winding mountain road. When it isn't blocked by snow you can also continue along the main road above Faraya to cross the barren ridges of Jebel Sannine and descend into the Bekaa Valley. ►► *For listings, see pages 70-72.*

Ins and outs

Getting there
There's no regular public transport to the Kesrouan region, but during the skiing season there are usually service taxis running from Dora Junction in Beirut to Faraya, and also between Faraya and the ski slopes at Mzaar.

If you're driving to the Kesrouan, head north from Beirut on the coastal motorway and 1 km after passing through the tunnel at Nahr el-Kalb, take the exit signposted clearly for Ajaaltoun, and less clearly for Jeita Grotto. If you are coming from Jounieh (heading south along the motorway) there is an exit and bridge across the motorway. The road climbs steeply from the motorway. After a little over 3 km there is a right turn signposted for **Jeita Grotto**. This side-road winds its way down into the picturesque Nahr el-Kalb Valley to arrive at the entrance to Jeita, 2.5 km away.

Continuing along the main road from the Jeita turning, after 9 km there is a right turn signposted for 'centre ville' just after you pass under a bridge; this takes you into the centre of the sprawling summer resort of **Aajaltoun**. There are a couple of hotels here, though other than the views out over the bay of Jounieh and the cooler climate in summer, there is little reason to stay. A little under 3 km from the turning for the centre of Aajaltoun, you come to a large roundabout. Bear right here to continue straight on (signposted 'Centres de Ski' on a Ministry of Tourism sign). A little under 4 km after the roundabout, there is a large fork off to the right (signposted to Kafr Debian and Faqra); this is the start of the alternative route via Kfar Debian to Faraya village, Mzaar and Faqra (see below).

Continuing straight on, after just under 3 km (immediately after La Rocha restaurant), there is a small left turn with a sign by it for 'La Reserve'. This turning joins the road leading up to Afqa Spring in the **Adonis Valley**. This is a beautiful route on a road lined with apple orchards and tomato fields and through stunning mountain scenery. Taking the turning, turn right at the top of the road (which forks just short of what is in effect a T-junction), bear left soon after (signposted to 'Qehmez') and keep going straight for 19 km. For an alternative route to the Adonis Valley, see page 73.

Carrying along the main road to Faraya, you pass through the village of **Mairouba** and, 12 km after the Afqa turning, you arrive at the roundabout in the centre of **Faraya**, passing the Coin Vert Hotel along the way.

Via Kfar Debian to Faraya, Mzaar and Faqra Taking the large fork off to the right as you come from Aajaltoun (signposted to Kafr Debian and Faqra), this road winds its way through dramatic mountain scenery before passing through the sprawling village of **Kfar Debian**. Just under 9 km from the fork (still in Kfar Debian), take the left turn signposted for 'Faqra Club' and then bear left wherever the road forks ambiguously. Just over 3 km further on you pass a major left turn; this road leads directly to the main route up to Mzaar resort and the village of Ouyoun es-Simaan just below, and Faqra resort and ski club.

Continuing straight on, after 1 km you pass though a checkpoint, and then 500 m further on you arrive at a crossroads and a sign for 'Archeologic sites of Faqra' (see below, under 'Faqra'). Continuing straight on again, after 1.5 km you pass the right turn up to Faqra Ski Club itself, followed 500 m further on by a natural rock bridge off to the left of the road. Another 1.5 km brings you to the junction/checkpoint on the road between Faraya and Mzaar; left leads around to Faraya, while right leads up to Mzaar resort and Ouyoun es-Simaan.

Faraya village and Mzaar Resort

During the winter the area around Faraya and Mzaar comes to life, with many people renting chalets and apartments for the whole season, and many more make the trip up from Beirut at the weekends. Without the snow, however, there is not very much to do, other than visit the dramatic ruins at Faqra. But it is a wonderfully serene and peaceful place to be during summer, and a welcome respite from the humidity of the coast. There are several hotels in and around Faraya, and directly below the Mzaar ski-lift centres in an area known as Ouyoun es-Simaan.

Ins and outs
Orientation The village of Faraya lies around 6 km below the actual ski resort, which is known as Mzaar or Ouyoun es-Simaan. The ski lifts to the slopes are about 1 km further on up the road. Turning left at the roundabout in the centre of Faraya, the road climbs steadily, before arriving at a checkpoint and junction after a little under 5 km. Turning

right at this junction takes you past the rock bridge, the turning for Faqra Ski Club, and the temple ruins of Faqra (see 'Faqra', below), while continuing straight on, you arrive soon after in Ouyoun es-Simaan and then, just above, the main Mzaar ski lift, known as Jonction. There is a second ski lift (called Wardeh) a further 2 km up the road.

Skiing at Mzaar

① Mon-Fri 0800-1530, Sat-Sun/public holidays 0800-1600, weekdays US$27, under 16-years US$20, weekends US$40, under 16-years US$30, weekdays half-day pass (after 1200), US$17, weekends half-day pass US$23.

This is Lebanon's most popular resort; it teems with people on the weekends, so plan to come on a weekday if you prefer a less crowded experience.

There are two main ski-lift stations, which provide access to slopes suitable for all levels of ability. **Jonction**, directly above Ouyoun es-Simaan, is the largest with eight lifts (one baby slope, three medium-ability slopes and four advanced slopes). Further up the road is **Wardeh**, where there are a further seven ski lifts leading to three baby slopes, two medium-ability slopes and two advanced slopes.

Visitors staying at the Mzaar Intercontinental Hotel have access to a third ski-lift centre, which operates from the hotel grounds. Known as the **Refuge**, this centre has two ski lifts both accessing medium level-slopes.

The 'Mzaar' chairlift at Jonction reaches the highest point of the resort (2465 m) from where there are stunning views out over the Bekaa Valley to the east, Mount Hermon to the south, Laqlouq and The Cedars to the north and the Mediterranean to the west. The resort has two snow machines that can be used on even the steepest slopes. Snowploughs are on hand to keep the main road up to the resort open throughout the season. Various skiing competitions are held from February to March and there is occasionally floodlit night skiing on the 'Refuge' slopes.

Skiing lessons can be arranged and ski equipment is available for hire at both Jonction and Wardeh as well as through the hotels in Faraya and Ouyoun es-Simaan. There are also a number of ski-hire shops in Faraya and on the main road between Aajaltoun and Faraya.

Mzaar to the Bekaa Valley

There is a wide, recently resurfaced road that climbs from Mzaar up over the northern slopes of Jebel Sannine. Having climbed steeply, it winds its way through a desolate, hilly upland plateau before starting to descend. Around 15 km from Mzaar (soon after you begin to descend), you pass through a checkpoint and the road then descends steeply, and stunning views of the Bekaa Valley spread out before you.

A little under 8 km further on you come to a roundabout/junction with a restaurant beside it. Bearing left, the road climbs again, crossing the mountains to arrive near Afqa, at the head of the Adonis Valley (Nahr Ibrahim); see page 73. Bearing right, the road continues to descend, passing through the village of **Hadet** and then through a second checkpoint, before arriving at a crossroads (just over 8 km from the junction/roundabout and restaurant) with yet another checkpoint. Turn right here to head towards Zahle, or left to intersect with the road between Baalbek and Bcharre. Going straight on, you can intersect with the main road between Rayak and Baalbek. Turning right, you pass through the village of **Nabi Rchade** and then after 5 km, in the village of **Chimstar**, turn left to pick up the main road, from where it is a further 21 km on to Zahle.

Faqra

There's no village here as such, except for the artificial 'village' of the Faqra Ski Club, which is a private members-only ski field. The surrounding scenery here is beautiful, though it is fast disappearing under a sea of chalet complexes. At the moment massive cranes dominate the skyline along the road to Faqra Ski Club, busy with all the new construction work going on.

Even if you can't ski at Faqra club itself, the short trip here from Faraya is worthwhile to visit the Faqra temple ruins and to see the bizarre natural rock bridge.

Skiing at Faqra Club
ⓘ *Mon-Fri 0800-1530, Sat-Sun/public holidays 0800-1600, weekdays US$12, weekends US$20.*
This is a private ski club complete with its own mini-village of privately owned chalets and a luxury hotel. The resort has one chairlift, two ski lifts and a baby ski lift, giving access to some 200 ha of slopes that are suitable for all levels of ability. To ski here you must be invited as the guest of a club member, although it may be possible to arrange to ski as a visitor here during the week when it is much quieter. Ring the hotel in advance to enquire.

Rock bridge
En route between Faraya and Mzaar, if you turn right at the checkpoint and junction (5 km from Faraya), after 1.5 km you come to a signpost for 'Pont Naturel Kfardebian', off to the right of the road. A short track takes you down to a rock bridge over a stream, looking for all the world as if it has been carved by hand, although in fact it is a natural feature, eroded by the forces of nature out of the limestone rock.

Faqra temple ruins
ⓘ *Daily 0900-sunset, 2000 LBP (though the site is often left open and the guard often not here).*
Continuing straight on, you arrive after 1.5 km at a crossroads and sign for 'Archeologic sites of Faqra'. Visible off to your right, up a short track, are the remains of a curious cube-shaped structure, heavily ruined though solidly built of huge stone blocks. This is known as the **Claudius tower** and a Greek inscription above the entrance states that it was rebuilt by the Emperor Claudius in AD 43-44 and dedicated to the 'very great god' (almost certainly Adonis).

The cube base was once topped by a stepped pyramid that has now all but completely collapsed. Inside, steps lead up onto the roof. Given its unusual design and the style of the stone blocks used in its construction, it seems likely that the building is actually much older than its inscription suggests. To the right of the track leading up to the Claudius tower is the base of an altar, while to the left of the track is another smaller altar that's been restored, with 12 miniature columns arranged like a mini *portico* supporting the altar top.

Turning left at the crossroads, 500 m away at the bottom of this road, are the more substantial remains of two **temples**, both within fenced-off enclosures. The larger temple (to your right as you enter) was probably also dedicated to Adonis. It is set amidst limestone rocks that have been eroded into bizarre fluted shapes and look almost as if they have themselves been carved by hand. In front of the temple is a squat structure of huge stone blocks that probably served as an altar. The walls of the temple enclosure or *temenos* are still largely intact, while, inside, extensive restoration work has been carried out, including the use of dubious amounts of concrete in the reconstruction of the six columns that formed the *portico* of the *cella*.

The smaller temple (to your left as you enter) was originally dedicated to the Syrian goddess Atargatis and later became identified with Astarte, before being partially dismantled in the Byzantine era to build a church. The basic outline of the temple still stands, consisting of a rectangular building divided into a large antechamber followed by a smaller inner sanctum. Low niches line the walls of the latter, while on the ground there is a large circular stone basin with carved decorations on it. Adjacent to the temple, the ten standing columns that can still be seen formed the nave of the church; carved on one of the fallen stones in the compound is a Byzantine cross.

The Kesrouan listings

For Sleeping and Eating price codes and other relevant information, see pages 9-10.

🛏 Sleeping

Faraya village and Mzaar Resort *p67*
Most of the accommodation is in the form of chalets and apartments that are rented out for the whole of the skiing season and are often booked up as much as 1 year in advance. The hotel accommodation fills up quickly during the season, particularly on weekends. Price categories below are for the high season. Substantial discounts (often as much as 50%) are available in the low season (this is basically when there is no snow; ie from around late Apr/early May until Nov/Dec).

During winter telephone lines are invariably broken by storms, so most of the hotels make use of mobile phone numbers (code 03) as well as landlines.
$$$$ Mzaar InterContinental, Ouyoun es-Simaan, T09-340100, www.intercontinental. com. This low-rise resort is a tasteful blend of wood and traditional stone and boasts direct access to the slopes with its own ski lifts. Everything you could need is here – excellent restaurants, bar, pool, gym and a luxurious spa, plus tonnes of sports and activities on offer. The rooms are flooded with light and have balconies and come with all the usual mod cons, though the decor is unfortunately rather bland. Note that the slightly cheaper standard rooms are near identical to the de luxe rooms except that they are a little further from the core of the hotel. During low season there are generally good discounts to be found.

$$$ Merab, Ouyoun es-Simaan, T09-341341, www.merabhotel.com. The stylish rooms at this wonderfully friendly and family-run place are cosy and comfortable and there are larger (and more expensive) suites for families. All come with satellite TV and minibar and most have small balconies. It's an excellent choice, with a good restaurant and a free morning shuttle to the slopes for guests. Recommended.
$$ Al Badre, Main Rd, Faraya village, T03-749 999, www.albadrhotel.com. This curiously designed hotel has welcoming management who are happy to help. Families or friends can stay in a 2-bedroom chalet (complete with kitchenette, satellite TV and log fire) where loads of dark wood has been used to create an alpine-cabin feel. The only complaint is that they're a little pokey for 4 people. There are cheaper split-level studio-style rooms upstairs (satellite TV, balcony) and even the smaller (and cheaper) ones still come with kitchenette, making them perfect for those trying to cut down costs by eating in. Recommended.
$$ Tamerland, Main Rd between Faraya and Ouyoun es-Simaan, T09-321268. Closed due to renovation work at the time of research, but should be open again by the time this book is published. This lovely big old building is set back from the road and surrounded with trees. Before the renovation the decently sized rooms here were a homely and quiet choice and each came with private balcony. There are also bigger (2 bedroom) apartments with kitchenettes that are excellent for families.
$ Coin Vert, Main Rd, Faraya, T09-321556, T03-724611, www.coin-vert.com. Stuck

in a 1970s time warp, when pine-wood clad interiors were the height of hotel chic, Coin Vert is Faraya's top budget choice. The rooms are nothing to write home about; small and a tad dreary with threadbare carpets and miniscule bathrooms, but they're clean and bright, with most possessing tiny balconies. Staff and management are helpful and smiley. Ask to see a few rooms before deciding as some are better than others. Member of the DHIAFEE hotel network. Recommended.

Faqra p69

$$$$ Auberge de Faqra, Faqra Ski Club, T09-300600, www.faqraclub.com. This large complex right by Faqra's slopes boasts a heated pool, restaurants, bar, spa/health club and access to all sorts of sport and activity facilities. The rooms are comfortable, though overpriced. Breakfast included.
$$$$-$$$ Terrebrune, on rd to Faqra Club, T09-300060, T03-030301, www. terrebrunehotel.com. This stylish and slick hotel is the height of modern luxury with its mix of traditional stone walls, neutral decor and snazzy low-lighting. The quiet rooms here (a/c, satellite TV, minibar, Wi-Fi) are large and swish with spacious bathrooms and either a terrace or balcony. There are lots of little extras to make your stay comfortable, with a good range of bath products in the bathroom and tea/coffee-making facilities in all rooms. The hotel is open all year and can arrange ATV and mountain-biking trips in summer. The outdoor pool has incredible views.

Eating

Faraya village and Mzaar Resort p67
All the hotels have restaurants; most of them offer inclusive full- or half-board deals, so there's not that much in the way of independent restaurants.

If you're after a snack or a cheap meal there are a few simple places on the main road in Faraya village. 2 of the better ones

are **Snack Bafaraya**, on the roundabout and **Quick Snack**, on the main road near the Coin Vert Hotel. If you feel like something different, the café inside **B Zone Internet**, opposite the Coin Vert Hotel, dishes up decent crêpes. Both the **supermarket** and **fruit and vegetable market** are on Faraya village's main road.

♯♯♯ Le Refuge, Mzaar InterContinental Hotel, Ouyoun es-Simaan. Top dining with an alpine twist. If you feel like going retro, the fondue here is popular and there are 6 delicious choices. The perfect end to a day on the slopes. Inside the hotel there's also a couple of other options: **La Tavola** (Italian) and **Les Airelles** (classic French cuisine).
♯♯♯ Pancho Vino, main rd, near Franzabank, Faraya village. This upmarket restaurant has a mix of dishes that span a range of different international cuisines, with steaks, pizza and various Mexican specialities all appearing on the menu. Portions are decent though it can be pricey.
♯♯ Chez Mansour, in front of the Merab Hotel, Ouyoun es-Simaan. A great little place under the same friendly management as the Merab Hotel. Cosy and welcoming, this is a top choice if you want hearty and no-nonsense food at good value prices close to the slopes. Recommended.
♯♯ Coin Vert, Coin Vert Hotel, main rd, Faraya village. Unpretentious dining and a decent budget option. There's a range of Lebanese and European dishes on offer, all at reasonable prices, in this simple and homely restaurant.
♯♯ Jisr al-Kmar, main road, near the roundabout, Faraya village. An excellent and reasonably priced restaurant that serves up good Lebanese staples (all your usual grills and meze) year-round with an outdoor terrace for lazy dining in the sun during summer months and cosy interior dining hall for when it's snowing outside.

Faqra p69
Inside the actual Faqra Ski Club there are various options, including the restaurants

inside the Auberge de Faqra Hotel.

♥♥♥ Chez Michel, off the main road just below the turning for Faqra Ski Club, T09-341021, T03-694462. This smart and stylish restaurant/bar attracts a pretty exclusive crowd, so dress to impress if you want to eat here. Open throughout the year, Chez Michel serves high-quality Lebanese cuisine. During the ski season it's a top party venue with live music or DJs on weekend nights.

❷ Entertainment

Faraya village and Mzaar Resort *p67*
Après-ski activity mostly revolves around Ouyoun es-Simaan, near the slopes. The bar in the **Mzaar Intercontinental Hotel** is a popular place to hang out and is open 24/7. Down in Faraya village the less pretentious **Kayak Club** is a great option for a drink.

❶ Directory

Faraya village and Mzaar Resort *p67*
Banks Fransabank, with ATM, main road, Faraya village. **Internet** B Zone Internet, opposite the Coin Vert Hotel. **Medical services** Services on the slopes during the ski season include an ambulance and qualified mountain rescue team, with an additional doctor and Red Cross team on weekends and holidays. There's a **pharmacy**, main road, Faraya village. **Telephone** Cardphones on the central roundabout and opposite the police station, Faraya village.

Adonis Valley
(Nahr Ibrahim Valley)

The Adonis Valley climbs steeply into the mountains to the east of Byblos. This region is the source of numerous extraordinary legends surrounding the cult of Adonis, and the setting for some interesting ancient ruins. The valley and the surrounding mountains are also stunningly beautiful, making it the perfect place for a leisurely day's drive through some of the best of Mount Lebanon's landscapes. There's no public transport, so if you want to explore you'll have to hire a car or a driver. ‣ *For listings, see page 77.*

Ins and outs

Getting there
Heading north on the coastal motorway from Beirut/Jounieh, take the Qartaba exit to join the road heading up to **Qartaba**. To join the Qartaba road from the old coast road, head south out of Byblos and through the villages of Fidar and Halat. Turn left to cross over the motorway and head up towards Qartaba (if you cross a stream – the Nahr Ibrahim – you have gone too far).

Heading north from Jounieh on the old coast road, having passed through the villages of Tabarja, Safra, Bouar and Aqaibé, take the right turn around 100 m after the bridge across the Nahr Ibrahim (a sign by the bridge announces the start of Nahr Ibrahim village).

The Qartaba road, rather busy and built up to begin with, climbs steeply into the mountains, with superb views west out over the Mediterranean coast. To the south, meanwhile, there are spectacular views down into the deep, sheer-sided gorge of the Nahr Ibrahim, and to the north occasional glimpses, equally spectacular, down into the Nahr el-Fidar. After 12 km you come to a checkpoint and right turn leading down to the village of Adonis. Continuing straight on, the road narrows considerably and after a further 10 km brings you to the tiny village of Machnaqa.

Machnaqa

The literal translation of this village name is 'place of the hanging'. Just before entering the village, you can see some **temple ruins** off to the right of the road, on a level-topped hill. A rough track leads past a tiny chapel (built partly of stones from the temple) up to the ruins. Alternatively, a little further along the road, a set of steps right by the signpost announcing the start of Machnaqa village leads up to the ruins, passing through a narrow cleft cut into the rocks with heavily weathered reliefs on either side (said to depict Adonis and Astarte but no longer clearly discernible). Dotted around are a number of trench-like tombs cut into the rocks.

Qartaba

From Machnaqa it is a further 11 km on to Qartaba, the road en route giving ever more dramatic, and at times extremely vertiginous, views down into the Nahr Ibrahim Valley. The small town of Qartaba is beautifully located, overlooking the valley, and is itself rather picturesque, with its large church and square, and substantial, well-built houses giving it a certain air of affluence. Surrounding the town are fertile olive groves, mulberry orchards and vineyards. There are a couple of seasonal hotels/restaurants in the town, making it a pleasant place to stay during the summer. The main road passes along the top of the town, which spreads down the hillside below. Entering the village, bear left where the road forks to keep to the upper road, and then bear right at the next junction (with an Esso garage beside it; left leads across to Laqlouq). Around 300 m further on, bear right down to the Rivola Hotel, or bear left for the road to Afqa.

Mugheir

A little under 6 km beyond Qartaba, you come to a set of **temple ruins** right by the road. The rectangular building, dating from Greek or Roman times and again most probably dedicated to Adonis, has three fairly well-preserved walls, with traces of its original decoration still visible. During the Byzantine period, the temple was converted into a church, with the missing fourth side of the building (originally the entrance) forming the apse.

The site is known locally as *Mar Jurios Azraq* (literally 'St George the Blue', the epithet 'the Blue' perhaps being derived from the greyish-blue granite from which the church was built). Surrounding the temple/church are the remains of a larger compound, built from huge blocks of reddish stone. Although the stones from which this compound has been constructed are certainly much older, in their present form they are thought to have been arranged as fortifications by the Crusaders during the 12th century.

Adonis Valley & Jebel Tannourine

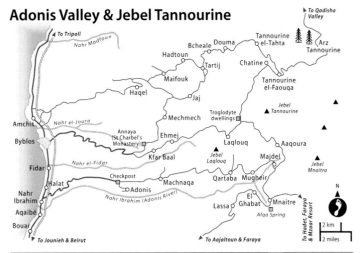

Majdel and Mnaitre

Continuing on from Mugheir, after 1.5 km you cross a stream on a small bridge (this is a tributary of the Nahr Ibrahim). A further 1.5 km after crossing the stream, there is a sharp right turn signposted 'La Reserve Afqa' (straight on is signposted 'Laklouk', this road passing first through Aaqoura to reach Laqlouq, see below).

Taking the sharp right turn, after a little under 3 km you come to a left turn signposted once again for 'La Reserve'. As well as taking you past the La Reserve camping/activity centre, this is the start of the road that crosses the high ridges of Mount Lebanon and descends into the Bekaa Valley (see below). Continuing straight on, it is a further 2.5 km to Afqa spring.

Shortly before you reach the spring, you pass through the tiny village of **Mnaitre**. This is where a Maronite missionary by the name of Abraham is said to have first settled when he came to Lebanon during the fifth century, and it was in his honour that the Adonis Valley was later named the Nahr Ibrahim. There are hot springs in the village, while up on a hilltop above the village there are traces of ruins, said by some to be the Crusader castle known as Le Moinestre, which was destroyed by Salah ud-Din in 1110.

Afqa

The scenery approaching Afqa is beautiful and dramatic. Arriving at the spring, you are confronted by enormous cliffs towering nearly 200 m above you, their sheer face broken by a huge cavern from which the Afqa spring, the source of the Nahr Ibrahim, gushes out in a forceful torrent. A rough path leads steeply up to the gaping opening; depending on the season (and therefore the level of the waters), if you can negotiate the unseemly tangle of pipes that emerge from it, you can scramble right up inside the cavern. The roof, noticeably uniform, shows signs of having been chiselled, and according to some sources there was originally a temple dedicated to Adonis inside the cavern itself. In Arabic the name Afqa translates as 'source', but in Greek Aphaca means literally 'the kiss'; this allegedly being the place where Adonis and Aphrodite first met and fell in love.

A little further along the road, to the right, a fenced-off area contains the tumbled ruins of a **temple**, its form no longer distinguishable, though the mass of scattered stones indicate that it must have been of substantial proportions. Exactly when it was first constructed is uncertain, though in legend it was Cinyrias, the king of Cyprus and father of Adonis, who built it. Whoever was responsible obviously went to great lengths, as the granite column discovered here, which must have been transported from Egypt, shows. Originally dedicated to Astarte, during Roman times its importance continued as a temple of Venus. Wishing to eradicate the licentious pagan cults that held such sway in this region, the Byzantine emperor Constantine ordered that it be destroyed. However, it was not until the end of the fourth century, during the reign of Arcadius, that it was finally reduced to ruins under the directions of St John Chrysostom.

At the base of the ruins there is an arched opening from which a small spring emanates, and which still serves as a shrine, with candles inside and bits of cloth tied to an overhanging fig tree. So Afqa remains a sacred site in the minds of local people. Christians identify it with the Virgin Mary and Shiite Muslims with a woman named *Zahra*, of uncertain origin, and both groups make pilgrimages to the site in search of fertility or cures for illnesses.

Heading down the hillside from the temple ruins, you get the best views back up to the cavern and spring, and also a good view of the old stone arched **bridge**, now contained within the larger arch of a later bridge.

The cult of Adonis

The cult of Adonis flourished in Byblos, and the Adonis Valley from Phoenician times. According to one Greek version of the legend, Adonis was the offspring of an incestuous relationship between Cinyrias, the king of Cyprus, and his daughter Myrrha. Famed for his good looks, Aphrodite, the goddess of love, soon fell in love with him and at Afqa they exchanged their first kiss. Her husband Ares (to the Romans, Mars), jealous of their love, caused a wild boar to attack Adonis while he was out hunting in the mountains of Lebanon. Mortally wounded, Adonis died in his lover's arms. Where his blood fell, crimson anemones sprung up (anemones are still known in Arabic as 'the wounds of Naaman', Naaman meaning 'darling' and being an epithet of Adonis). Aphrodite, inconsolable at her loss, petitioned the god Zeus (Roman Jupiter) to allow her to be reunited with Adonis, either through her own death or else by his resurrection. Eventually a compromise was reached whereby Adonis was allowed to leave the underworld for half of each year,

providing he returned for the remainder. Thus, every spring, Adonis was born again into the world and reunited with Aphrodite, only to die again in autumn.

Although on the surface a love story, the legend also clearly has its roots in those primordial themes of fertility, death and rebirth. Adonis is closely identified by some with vegetation, visibly prosperous during the six favourable months of the year, and lurking hidden under the cold ground during the remainder. Others see evidence of a sun myth in which Adonis, the short-lived sun, is slain by the boar, the demon of darkness, and passionately mourned by the dawn or twilight (Venus), who utterly refuses to live without him. With the advent of Christianity, the cult of Adonis was banned, but found new life in the form of St George, ever popular in Lebanon. Astarte-Aphrodite-Venus, meanwhile, became identified with the Virgin Mary. It has also been suggested that the Christian festival of Easter, celebrating the resurrection of Christ, may have replaced the pagan celebration of the resurrection of Adonis.

Aaqoura and the road to Laqlouq

Coming from Qartaba, if you continue straight on past the turning for Afqa, the road runs along the east side of the picturesque tributary valley of the Nahr Ibrahim, arriving after just over 3 km at Aaqoura. Nestling beneath towering cliffs of sheer rock, the village of Aaqoura is an important Maronite centre, with numerous churches and shrines, including one dedicated to Mar Butros (St Peter), which is perched in a natural grotto in the cliff face and reached by a steep stairway cut into the rock.

The grotto, with its hollowed-out tombs cut into the rock, appears to have originally been a Roman necropolis before being converted into a Christian shrine. At the back of the grotto, faint traces of the rare *Estrangelo* script can be seen, painted in red on the rock. This vertical Syriac script is thought to have been developed by Nestorean Christian missionaries who visited China in the seventh century and adopted elements of the Chinese script.

Continuing on from Aaqoura, the road climbs steadily and the mountains begin to open out. After just over 5 km you come to a very sharp right turn, followed 300 m further on by a very sharp left turn. Another 1 km brings you to a second sharp right turn; this is the start of the road to Tannourine el-Faouqa. The rather vaguely and confusingly aligned signpost by the junction reads 'St Charbel-Annanaya 14 km'. Continuing straight on, just past the junction there is a signpost announcing, equally confusingly, the start of Ehmej; in fact you are approaching the ski resort of Laqlouq (see page 79), Ehmej is some distance further down the valley.

The road across to the Bekaa Valley

Take the signposted turning for La Reserve 2.5 km to the north of Afqa spring. This excellent road climbs steeply up, heading east, with ever more vertiginous views down the valley, before winding through an upland plateau of hills. After 14 km you pass through a checkpoint, and then around 1 km further on begin to descend, with panoramic views of the Bekaa Valley.

Some 5 km after the checkpoint (and 1 km after passing a sharp right turn), you arrive at a roundabout/junction with a restaurant beside it. Bearing right here takes you back up over the mountains to Mzaar, while bearing left takes you down into the Bekaa Valley.

Adonis Valley (Nahr Ibrahim Valley) listings

For Sleeping and Eating price codes and other relevant information, see pages 9-10.

☺ Sleeping and eating

Qartaba *p74*
$ Rivola, T09-405002. Open May-Oct (depending on weather, phone to check). This friendly family-run hotel is set in a big old house with simple but comfortable rooms with attached balconies offering lovely views out over the valley. Restaurant.

Mugheir *p74*
$ Al Rabih Motel, between Mugheir and Majdel, to the right of the road down by the stream, just before you cross the bridge, T03-249051. Open Apr-Oct (phone to check). Simple but clean and pleasant rooms with balconies provide lovely views out over the stream and down the valley. The restaurant serves fresh trout from its own trout pools.

Afqa *p75*
$ La Reserve, taking the signposted turning for 'La Reserve' 2.5 km to the north of Afqa spring, the camp is off to the right, 400 m further on, T03-727484, www.lareserve.com. lb. Open May-Oct (phone to check). The awesome mountain scenery and stunning views make this a truly dramatic wilderness camping location. You can pitch your own tent or use one of the reserve's own permanent tents, which sleep up to 4 people and come with bedding, lighting and even a power socket for your mobile phone. There are clean shower/toilet facilities (and hot water) and also a café/restaurant. Activities include archery, horse riding, mountain biking, abseiling, potholing, canoeing and rafting.

Jebel Tannourine

There are several interesting and extremely scenic trips that can be made from Byblos into the mountains. The most obvious route is the one leading due east up to the monastery and shrine of St Charbel at Annaya, and then via the village of Ehmej to the ski resort of Laqlouq. From Laqlouq there are several options. One road leads via the village of Aaqoura down to Qartaba, with the possibility of diverting to Afqa, while another continues north to Tannourine el-Faouqa, from where you can either head across to the Qadisha Valley, or else round to the pretty town of Douma and then return via a winding mountain road to the coast at Amchit, just north of Byblos. ‣ *For listings, see page 82.*

Ins and outs

Getting there
Heading in either direction along the coastal motorway, take the Byblos exit. Coming from the old coast road in the centre of Byblos, follow the dual carriageway with the remains of the Roman street running along the centre and cross over the coastal motorway. From here, a broad highway climbs up through Byblos' suburbs and into the mountains. Higher up, there are lots of snack bars and small restaurants strategically placed to make the most of the panoramic views out over the Mediterranean.

Some 14.5 km after crossing over the motorway, you arrive at a checkpoint and junction, preceded by several more restaurants as well as a number of shops lining the road; fork left here to make a short detour up to the monastery and shrine of **St Charbel** at Annaya (a little over 2 km further on, see below), or right to head towards Laqlouq.

Bearing right, the broad highway continues through the village of Kfar Baal up to the town of **Ehmej**, which spreads out for a couple of kilometres along the road. From Ehmej onwards, the road up to Laqlouq is undergoing major improvements to update and widen it and, at the time of research, was still a narrow, unsurfaced lane for most of the way, with lots of road works happening. From the church that marks the approximate centre of Ehmej (6 km from the checkpoint and junction), it is a further 6 km up to the lower section of **Laqlouq**, the valley gradually narrowing as you ascend.

St Charbel Monastery

ⓘ *A private taxi from Byblos should not cost more than US$10-15 for the round trip, although this depends on the length of time you expect them to wait. On Sun there is a good chance of finding a service taxi heading up there from Byblos, or you could try hitching.*
Although first established in the early part of the 19th century, there have been substantial later additions to the monastery. Today, a visit is interesting more for the somewhat bizarre experience of seeing a flourishing modern-day Maronite pilgrimage centre in action, rather than for the building itself.

Inside the monastery there is a small museum where various items from St Charbel's life are displayed, including piles of crutches belonging to those cured by his miracles, the papal letter of canonization, pieces of his blood-stained clothing and a tacky display of mannequins depicting his family praying before a meal.

There are no less than three tombs for the Saint, his remains having been transferred to a new one each time they were disinterred. The devout can also obtain pieces of cloth stained with the blood that is said to still issue from his body. A souvenir shop sells all sorts of St Charbel-related souvenirs, while opposite the monastery there is another shop selling locally produced wine. Unfortunately, the rapid development of the area and the rather crude commercialization of the monastery as a pilgrimage site have robbed it of the sense of solitude and isolation that must have existed in St Charbel's lifetime.

You can get to the nearby hilltop **hermitage** to which he retreated by following the signs from the monastery, rather than the fork soon after the checkpoint and junction. Though it still has something of a pilgrimage theme park atmosphere about it, it does retain something of its original tranquillity along with spectacular views out over the Mediterranean.

Laqlouq Ski Resort

ⓘ *Mon-Fri 0800-1530, Sat-Sun 0800-1600, weekdays US$16, under 15-years US$13, weekends US$23, under 15-years US$20, weekdays half-day pass (after 1200) US$11, weekends half-day pass US$15. On weekends during the winter skiing season, it may be possible to find service taxis running to Laqlouq from Byblos or from Dora Junction in Beirut, but otherwise the only way to get here is by your own transport or a private taxi.*

The ski resort of Laqlouq doesn't really have a centre as such; the first part you come to consists of the **Lavalade Hotel** and several chalet developments. Some 2 km further on, the **Shangri La Hotel** is signposted off to the right of the road. This hotel complex is close to the foot of the slopes, and there are a number of private chalet complexes nearby.

Originally Laqlouq was one of the smallest ski resorts in Lebanon alongside Qanat Bakich, but following development of the resort in 1996-1997 there are now three chair-lifts, three ski lifts and three baby lifts. Most of the slopes are quite gentle (suitable for beginners to medium ability), although one technical alpine slope has been approved by the International Ski Federation as suitable for Giant Slalom events at international competition level. There are also excellent opportunities for cross-country skiing.

As always, weekends are the busiest (and most expensive times) to ski. The ski school includes French instructors and has a good reputation. Skiing equipment is available for hire from between US$5-12 from shops on the road approaching the ski station and there are rescue and medical facilities on hand.

Routes from Laqlouq

If you continue up past the turning for the Shangri La hotel, after just under 1 km you come to a junction; bear left for Tannourine el-Faouqa (signposted for 'Tannourine', amongst others) or continue straight on (signposted rather confusingly 'Laklouk') to head down to Aaqoura and then Qartaba, passing en route the turning for Afqa. Bearing left, after 600 m you come to a striking cluster of protruding limestone rocks eroded into weird shapes beside the road. Cut into these rocks are tiny **troglodyte dwellings** of uncertain origin. They were once used as an army barracks but are now deserted.

Continuing on, you pass the village of Chatine, clinging prettily to a steep-sided rocky outcrop off to the left of the road, before arriving in a fork in the centre of the village of **Tannourine el-Faouqa**, 9 km from the junction above Laqlouq, from where you can visit the **Tannourine Cedar Nature Reserve**. The fork off to the left (signposted to Batroun and Tannourine el-Tahta, amongst others) leads to **Douma**. The fork off to the right leads across to the Qadisha Valley; around 100 m further on, bear round to the right in front of a large, grand-looking church, then go left immediately afterwards. Start asking directions through the village from here – picking up the correct road is rather tricky.

The road across to the Qadisha Valley is spectacularly beautiful. It climbs steeply from Tannourine el-Faouqa and then follows a wide arc around the head of a valley before descending to Hadath el-Jobbe (18 km). This road has been resurfaced, making it an extremely pleasant alternative approach to Bcharre and well worth doing if you have your own transport.

Tannourine Cedar Nature Reserve

ⓘ *T06-500 550, www.arztannourine.org, daily 0800-1800, 5000 LBP. To get trail maps of the reserve and find out information, you can either visit the Reserve Office (located in the centre of Tannourine el-Faouqa village, daily 0800-1700) or ask at the info booth at the reserve entrance (daily 0800-1800, Apr-Nov).*

Protected since 1999, this tiny nature reserve (covering only 12 km) contains one of the largest and densest stands of cedar trees in the country. Tannourine is an excellent hiking destination due to the nature reserve's mountainous terrain, and is also home to many rare plants endemic only to high altitude environments. The best time to come here is the flowering season of March to October when the reserve is at its most colourful.

Trail 1 (2 km, one hour, medium) is the main walking path from the entrance and gives a good overview of the reserve's forests, passing through stands of cedar, maple, oak and juniper trees. It ends at Wadi Ain al Fouar from where you can pick up other paths, head back to the main entrance or be picked up in a vehicle.

Trail 4 (4 km, 2½ hours, medium-hard) is a circular trail beginning from the main entrance and passing through Wadi Ain al Fouar and the scenic high point of Ras al Wadi. Hikers have abundant opportunity to view the alpine flora of the reserve as well as some great views.

Trail 5 (2 km, one hour, medium) begins at Wadi Ain al Fouar and makes an excellent, and not too difficult, extension to Trail 1. The dense forest along this stretch and the many different flowers (during flowering season) make it a particularly beautiful walk. It ends at the main road from where you can be picked up in a vehicle.

Trail 6 (4.5 km, 2½ hours, hard) is also a good extension to Trail 1 if you feel like a harder hike. This trail traverses through the forest up to the nature reserve's high point at Ras al Wadi, from where you are rewarded with brilliant views over the surrounding countryside.

Douma

Douma is unique in that it has largely escaped the modern concrete construction you find practically everywhere else in Lebanon. Instead, the town has managed to preserve its beautiful Ottoman period houses with their distinctive red-tiled roofs. With strictly enforced town planning regulations, it has also managed for the most part to preserve a distinctive scorpion-shape layout, clearly discernible when viewed from above.

The town's name is said to be derived from Julia Domna, the wife of the Roman Emperor Septimus Severus (AD 193-211), who supposedly used it as a summer retreat. During the

The Cedars of the Lord

Known locally as *Al Arz al-Rab* (The Cedars of the Lord), the Lebanese Cedar is the country's national symbol, and a source of great pride amongst the Lebanese. Once, much of the Lebanon mountain range was clad in rich cedar forests (conservative estimates suggest that these would have covered as much as 80,000 ha), but their exploitation goes back just about as far as recorded history.

According to legend, Gilgamesh, the third millennium BC king of Uruk in southern Mesopotamia, came to Lebanon to cut down cedars for his city. Inscriptions discovered at Mari in Syria relate how the Amorite king Yakhdun Lim did likewise in the second millennium BC, while the campaign history of Tiglath Pilser I, the late second millennium BC Assyrian king, tell a similar story. There are also numerous references in the Bible to the exploitation of Lebanon's cedar forests by the Phoenicians of Tyre, Sidon and Byblos, both for the building of ships and for export to Egypt and Israel. Most famously, the Bible recounts how King Solomon's temple in Jerusalem was built of cedar wood beams, and panelled throughout with cedar, "*So give orders that cedars of Lebanon be cut for me... So Solomon built the temple and completed it... The inside of the temple was cedar, carved with gourds and open flowers. Everything was cedar; no stone was to be seen.*" (1 Kings 5; 6, 9, 1 Kings 6; 14, 18)

The exploitation continued more or less unabated through the Roman, Byzantine and Islamic periods, right up until the trees felled by the Ottomans for use as sleepers in the building of the Hejaz railway, and during the First World War as fuel on the trains. Today, despite attempts to regenerate the remaining stands of cedars through planting schemes, there is evidence to suggest that they are under serious stress from pollution, soil erosion and infection, and that their ability to survive naturally in such small numbers is debatable.

Ottoman period the town flourished as a centre for the production of swords and guns, with the inhabitants using the wealth they accumulated to build the grand red-roofed houses that can be seen today. Although there is nothing of special interest in Douma, it is a picturesque town with several pleasant cafés in the centre, where the local men come to pass the time drinking tea and coffee, smoking *narghiles* and playing *towleh* (the Arab version of backgammon). There are also plenty of opportunities for hiking in the surrounding hills (the **Douma** hotel organizes hiking trips).

Douma back to the coast

Coming from the Douma hotel, turn left in the centre of Douma. The road climbs steeply from here, with various vantage points giving excellent views of the town and its distinctive scorpion shape spread out below. After crossing a watershed, the road descends through strikingly eroded limestone rock formations, passing through the village of **Bcheale** (a little over 3 km from Douma), also notable for its red-roofed houses, before arriving in **Tartij**, 5 km further on. Turn right in the centre of Tartij (marked by a statue of St George slaying the dragon, and signposted for Hadtoun, Maifrouk and Aale) to pick up the road leading down to the coast at Amchit.

The road leading down into **Maifouk** takes you past numerous tombs and the chapel of St Elije. The centre of the village is marked by a mini-roundabout with a hand-like sculpture in the centre. Bearing right here brings you to the entrance to a large monastery and school, also dedicated to St Elije (the 'Monastery of Our Lady of Maifouk'). In its present form this dates from 1904. Opposite is a tiny chapel that was part of the original monastery.

Bear left at the mini-roundabout in Maifouk to continue on towards Haqel. Around 3 km beyond Maifouk, you pass a fork off to the left signposted to Jaj and St Charbel's Monastery (Annaya). Keep going straight and, 2 km further on, follow the road round sharply to the left (ignoring a right turn on the bend signposted in Arabic only) to descend into a narrow valley. The road crosses the valley's stream near its head (look out for the remains of an old dry-stone bridge by the stream) then loops around to the right to double back along the opposite (south) side before arriving in **Haqel**, 7 km from Maifouk and 22 km from Douma.

The valley here is famous for its marine fossils and there are a couple of shops in the village selling stones with the fossilized skeletons of fish imprinted on them, ranging in size from a few centimetres up to a metre and more. The presence of such fossils at this altitude (600 m) is evidence of the fact that during the cretacian and cenomanian eras (90-110 million years ago) most of Lebanon was immersed under the sea.

The road continues along the south side of the valley, which develops steadily into a deep gorge, passing through a number of small villages. Keep going straight, descending through the old part of Amchit. Around 16 km from Haqel you cross over the coastal motorway, before joining the old coast road 2 km to the north of Byblos.

Jebel Tannourine listings

For Sleeping and Eating price codes and other relevant information, see pages 9-10.

⊜ Sleeping and eating

St Charbel Monastery *p78*
There are dozens of restaurants down by the checkpoint and junction and along the road leading to the monastery.
$ Oasis St Charbel, right next door to the monastery, T09-760241. Run by the monastery itself and, although really only meant for bona fide pilgrims, this hostel is also open to any other travellers who wish to stay here. The simple (going on spartan) rooms are spotlessly clean and all have attached bathrooms. There's a restaurant right beside the hostel.

Laqlouq ski resort *p79*
There are a couple of snack places at the foot of the slopes (open during the winter only), but otherwise the only restaurants are those attached to the hotels.
$$$ Shangri La, Laqlouq, T03-441112, www.lakloukresort.com. This pleasant, old-style hotel has friendly management and is geared very much towards families. The rooms are

nothing special, but they're clean and quite spacious. A full range of ski equipment can be hired here and during the summer the hotel can arrange ATV and mountain bike hire.

Tannourine Cedar Nature Reserve *p80*
$$ Sarkis Guesthouse, Tannourine el-Faouqa, T03-679055. A genuine Lebanese experience. Although it won't suit everyone, this cheerful little family home has opened up its doors to travellers with the delightful Sarkis family as your hosts. Services and amenities are basic with the super-clean simple rooms all sharing bathrooms. All meals (good old-fashioned hearty fare) can be provided, and your hosts can help arrange hikes and other activities in the nature reserve. There is no English spoken. Member of the DHIAFEE hotel network.

Douma *p80*
$$ Douma, T06-520202, www.hoteldouma.com. A friendly and well-run hotel built in art-deco circular style that sits rather incongruously among Douma's traditional architecture. Rooms all come with satellite TV, Wi-Fi and balconies with great views. There's a decent restaurant here as well.

Qadisha Valley and The Cedars

The Qadisha is the heartland of the Maronite Christian community and one of the most beautiful regions in the country. The superb hiking opportunities available here make it a must-do for any keen trekker. Not far from here, sitting in the shadow of Lebanon's highest peak is The Cedars; one of Lebanon's most popular ski resorts and home to the tiny stand of cedar trees that gave the town its name.

From the fertile Khoura plains that spread inland around Batroun, the Qadisha Valley climbs steeply in a a deep gorge that dramatically slashes through the mountainside. Clinging precariously to the surrounding slopes, surrounded by an amphitheatre of mountains, are charmingly quaint villages where little seems to have changed for 100 years. Here, among the narrow streets of cottages with their colourful wooden window shutters and tiny pavement flower gardens, life slows down to a snail's pace. Old men gather outside the village café to watch the world go by, farmers chug down the middle of the road on beaten-up tractors and elderly women sit for hours in front of their houses gossiping. This is Lebanese mountain life at its prettiest and it won't be long before you have fallen under its spell.

Budget travellers will be happy to know that not only is this area accessible by public transport but the main centre for travellers, Bcharre, also has decent, cheap accommodation options. ↦ *For listings, see pages 96-100.*

Ins and outs

Getting there

The Qadisha Valley has excellent public transport connections with Tripoli. Regular buses journey from Tripoli via the valley's southern rim all the way to Bcharre. The northern rim of the valley is not serviced by public transport and you'll need a car/driver if you want to explore it. If you're driving, there are several routes you could take to get here, see below.

The route through the Khoura from the coast

Heading north on the coastal motorway, the exit for Chekka and Amioun (signposted for Ehden, The Cedars and Chekka) is just after a checkpoint, 6 km beyond the tunnel through the promontory of Ras ech-Chekka (see page 95). Heading north on the old coast road, after the tunnel through the promontory of Ras ech-Chekka, the road descends past various small beach resorts; the right turn for Amioun is just under 1 km beyond the left turn signposted for the Palmara resort.

Heading south on the coastal motorway, the Chekka/Amioun exit is 18 km from the start of the motorway in Tripoli, just before you reach the checkpoint. Heading south on the old coast road, the turning for Amioun (not signposted) is the first left turn you come to immediately after leaving Chekka. After leaving/crossing over the motorway, a good road climbs gently up through the fertile Khoura plain, passing through rich olive groves and orchards. A little over 5 km from the motorway, go straight at a crossroads and checkpoint. From here it's 4 km into the centre of Amioun.

Amioun

Amioun, at an altitude of 400 m, is the principal town of the Koura region, and has a predominantly Greek Orthodox population. As you approach the centre, above the road to the left you can see a chapel on top of a rocky outcrop, with lots of small, square chambers cut into the rock below. This is **St John's chapel** ('Mar Youhanna') a relatively recent construction, while the rock-cut chambers below it are burial vaults dating from the Roman period, or perhaps even earlier. Spread out over this long, narrow outcrop of rock is the old village of Amioun, which is well worth exploring.

To get up to it, turn left at the traffic lights around 200 m beyond St John's chapel and the burial vaults and take the small left turn around 200 m further on. Although the first part is accessible by car, the road is extremely steep and it is best to go on foot. Wandering around the narrow streets, you can forget for a moment all the glitzy new development that lines the modern road (itself only constructed in 1986) and get a glimpse of the quiet, parochial atmosphere that once would have reigned in this small village.

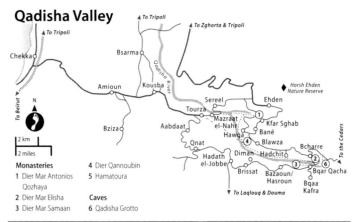

Qadisha Valley

Monasteries
1 Dier Mar Antonios Qozhaya
2 Dier Mar Elisha
3 Dier Mar Samaan

4 Dier Qannoubin
5 Hamatoura

Caves
6 Qadisha Grotto

Sights In the old village of Amioun there is a fascinating blend of old Ottoman architecture mixed in with more modern construction, the latter often built straight onto the former. The size of many of the old houses gives an indication of the wealth generated by the olive-based economy of the village during the Ottoman period.

At the far end of the ridge is the large **Church of St George** ('Mar Gorjius'). This appears to have been built from an earlier Roman temple, as can be seen from the large stone blocks used in the lower courses of the walls, as well as the sections of columns laid horizontally as reinforcement. Higher up, the walls are of smaller, more recent stones while the bell tower is clearly a recent addition. The interior is plain vaulted with a stone *iconostasis* decorated with numerous painted icons in front of the apse. Flanking the apse there are two Roman columns, the capital of the left-hand one with a carved face still discernible on it.

In the centre of the village there are a couple more churches, and the austere-looking **Church of St Phocas** ('Mar Fauqa'), probably built in the 12th century by the Crusaders. Inside, the walls are decorated with Byzantine-style frescos dating from the 12th and 13th century.

Bziza

Around 500 m past the traffic lights and crossroads in the centre of Amioun, there is a right turn signposted for the village of Bziza (amongst others), 5 km away; ask directions along the way as the route is not very clear. Nearby are the remains of a **Roman temple**, dedicated originally to the Semitic god Azizos. The four limestone columns that formed the portico of the temple are still standing, three of them still topped by Ionic capitals and supporting the original architrave. Beyond the portico, the doorway of the temple is also well preserved, complete with its entire crowning entablature. During the Byzantine period, a church was erected within the temple.

Kousba

Returning to the main road and continuing east, turn left around 3 km after the crossroads and traffic lights in the centre of Amioun (signposted for Ehden). Go straight across the crossroads 1 km further on, in Kousba, another predominantly Greek Orthodox village and important market centre.

Hamatoura monastery The Greek Orthodox Hamatoura monastery is built precariously into the almost sheer cliff face, and is accessible only on foot (by means of a zig-zagging trail and steps leading up from the valley floor). The rock strata in the cliffs angle sharply upwards from the valley floor and then bend around in a broad arc, graphically revealing the geological processes of uplift and folding that formed these mountains.

According to some estimates, the monastery may have been established as early as the fourth century. At its height, during the 14th century, there were some 200 monks in residence here, though following a massacre at the hands of the Mamluks, it went into decline. In 1850 the Ottomans bombed the monastery, causing serious damage and killing 50 monks, while in 1917 it suffered further damage due to an earthquake. Since 1994, the Abbot, Father Pandelemion, has overseen its gradual restoration.

To reach the start of the trail up to the monastery, around 700 m after the crossroads in Kousba there is a small left turn. Follow this narrow road as it winds its way down to the bottom of the valley (around 2.5 km). The road ends at a hydroelectric station and a bridge across the river giving access to the trail and steps leading up to the monastery (a steep 30- to 45-minute climb).

When you get there, you pass through a short section of tunnel running under a newly constructed wing. The monastery's tiny chapel is partly built into the cliff face. Carved into the stonework above the entrance to the chapel is a Crusader-style cross (with twin horizontal members), while carved above the entrance to a cave behind the chapel is a Byzantine cross. Inside the chapel, there are a few small fragments of frescos, revealed after a fire in 1993 caused the plaster covering the walls to peel and flake. The frescos are all 10th century in style, except for one, which is thought to date from the sixth century.

From Kousba to Bcharre
Continuing east along the main road, 4 km beyond the turning for the Hamatoura monastery, you come to a checkpoint and fork in the road. If you fork right, the road climbs up over a shoulder of mountain, passing through the villages of **Aabdaat** (or Aabdine) and **Qnat**, off to the right of the road, before descending to **Hadath el-Jobbe** and continuing on to **Bcharre**.

Forking left, the road descends through the red-roofed villages of **Tourza** and **Mazraat el-Nahr**, before crossing the stream of the Qadisha Valley (3 km from the checkpoint). From here on, the valley is spectacularly beautiful. The road climbs, gently at first and then more steeply, to arrive at a mini-roundabout in **Sereel**, 2.5 km further on. Turn right here, and after a further 4 km you pass a right turn signposted to the 'Couvent St Antoine Kosbaiya' (this is the road leading down to Deir Mar Antonios Qozhaya, see page 93).

Bcharre

Dramatically located near the head of the Qadisha Valley, perched on the edge of sheer cliffs that plunge down to the valley floor, the town of Bcharre is famous for being the birthplace of Khalil Gibran, Lebanon's most famous poet. This pretty village, with its laid-back atmosphere, wonderfully quaint architecture and good accommodation options, is the obvious base from which to explore the stunningly beautiful Qadisha Valley. The Cedars (*Al Arz*) is also within easy reach.

Ins and outs
Getting there Bcharre is well serviced by public transport from Tripoli, all of which drops off passengers beside Mar Saba church in Bcharre's main square. There are regular buses and minibuses from Tripoli (travelling via the southern rim of the Qadisha Valley), about every 30 minutes in the morning and every hour in the afternoon. Service taxis are less frequent (except in peak summer and peak ski season, when you shouldn't have to wait long for a departure) and you'll have to wait for them to fill up before they leave.

Getting around The village itself is easily manageable on foot. To the east, just past the waterfall, a turning up the hillside is clearly signposted to the Gibran Museum, Notre Dame de Lourdes Grotto and Phoenician Tomb, all within walking distance. It's possible to walk down into the Qadisha Valley directly from Bcharre, or there is a road leading down to the valley floor from the south rim. You can also walk to the Qadisha Grotto and The Cedars (*Al Arz*) or, if you're not feeling in the mood for an 8-km hike uphill, there are private taxis available in the centre of the village.

Sights

Within Bcharre itself, two large churches stand out clearly from a distance: **Mar Saba church**, in the centre by the main square, is the largest, while a short way up from it is the **Virgin Mary church**. A third church to the west of St Saba along the main street is now a school.

In a small garden at the top of the main square, opposite Mar Saba church, is **Khalil Gibran's house**, the exterior of which has been restored, although there is nothing to see inside.

Khalil Gibran Museum ① *T06-671137, daily 1000-1800 in summer, Tue-Sun 1000-1600 in winter, 5000 LBP. Postcards, posters and framed prints of Gibran's paintings are on sale.*
The Gibran Museum, with its excellent views out over the Qadisha Valley, has the most beautiful setting and brings together an extensive collection of Khalil Gibran's (1883-1931) paintings and drawings, some 440 in all, of which 170 are displayed. Known primarily in the West for his poetry, in particular the book *The Prophet*, his paintings and drawings are in themselves remarkable and certainly merit greater recognition (although some critics point to their uncanny similarity to the works of William Blake). There is also some of his furniture and personal effects on display, while down a flight of stairs leading to one of the caves is his tomb, furnished with some more of his personal effects, including his bed and a large painted fabric alter-piece of the crucifixion that he was particularly fond of because it depicted Jesus smiling.

The history of the building is varied and interesting. From around the seventh century followers of Mar Sarkis (St Sergius) lived in the caves here and in time also built a hermitage. In the 15th century a small residence was erected for the Papal Nuncio (representative), which later expanded, along with the caves and hermitage, to become a monastery. In the 16th century it became the summer residence of the French Consul, and then in the 17th century it was donated to the Carmelite monks of the area. The present buildings date from this time and the monastery was then bought by Gibran who intended to use it as a retirement retreat. However, he died shortly afterwards and so it became instead a museum for his works, as well as his tomb.

Notre Dame de Lourdes Grotto Just behind the museum a footpath leads up a short distance to a small cave and spring dedicated to the Virgin Mary known as Notre Dame de Lourdes Grotto. According to legend, the location of the spring was revealed to one of the Carmelite monks in a vision by Mary, who took pity on the monk having to carry water all the way up to the monastery each day in order to irrigate his small vegetable garden.

Phoenician tomb Further up along the same path is a Phoenician tomb, consisting of a large conical obelisk of rock rising up out of the hillside (presumably carved into its present shape), with a chamber cut into its base and compartments inside for four coffins. The structure is thought to date from 750 BC.

Qadisha Grotto ① *6.5 km from the centre of town: take the right-hand turn signposted to 'Qadisha Grotto' around 2 km from Bcharre centre, on the road to The Cedars. This leads you up the winding old Cedars road. Follow the road as far as the L'Aiglion Hotel (3 km further on) and take the signposted footpath opposite (1.5 km), which leads to the grotto. Daily 0800-1700, closes with the first snows and remains closed until spring (usually Dec-May), 5000 LBP.* From the turn-off at the L'Aiglion Hotel, a narrow path traverses the mountainside with excellent views down into the Qadisha Valley, the last sections passing through tunnels cut into the rock face, before reaching the entrance to the grotto, where there is a simple restaurant.

The grotto is the source of the Qadisha River, which gushes out of the rock face in a powerful torrent. A natural tunnel carved out by the water extends for around 500 m into the side of the mountain, at the end of which there is a large cave with some interesting stalagmites and stalactites. Although no match in size for the Jeita Grotto, the strange and eerie limestone formations here, especially in the end cavern, are quite impressive, and wandering inside the grotto is a deliciously cold experience on a hot day. The views from the restaurant area outside are simply superb.

Exploring the Qadisha Valley from Bcharre

The deep gorge of the Qadisha Valley is an excellent place for walking, combining spectacularly beautiful natural scenery with some of the most important religious centres of the Maronite faith. There are numerous paths (some rather precarious) leading down into the valley at various points, and numerous isolated grottoes, hermitages, chapels and monasteries, but you really need a local guide to find many of these.

The main route down to the valley floor is accessible by car on a good road, minimizing the amount of walking needed. This is also the easiest (though longest) access point for walkers.

Deir Mar Elisha (St Elisée or St Eliseus)

This monastery began its life as an extremely basic hermits' retreat that originally occupied the caves in the rock face. Written evidence of Deir Mar Elisha as a functioning monastery, and indeed as the seat of a Maronite bishop, goes back to 1315, while artefacts discovered during restoration work in 1991 suggest that it may already have been in existence by the late 11th or early 12th century. Various phases of enlargement, modification and restoration have been identified during the 16th, 17th and early 20th centuries. Of great significance to Maronites is the fact that the Lebanese Maronite Order, the first formal Maronite religious order (initially known as the Aleppines, after its founders, who came from Aleppo), was founded here in 1695 and officially sanctioned by the Patriarch Stephen Douweihy in 1700.

The monastery's current chapel, to the right of the main entrance, was completed in 1835. Just inside the entrance to the monastery, steps lead up to a small grotto that formed part of a much earlier chapel and today houses the tomb of François de Chasteuil, a respected Capuchin, or Franciscan friar, who died here in 1644. The main body of the monastery stretches off to the left of the entrance and consists of a series of monks' cells on two levels. Today the monastery is in effect a museum, with information boards (in Arabic, French and English) detailing its various special features, and aspects of its history and that of the Maronite church in general. On the lower level you can see a small basin cut into the rock to collect water dripping from the rock face above, a much older entrance to the hermitage, a monk's hiding hole and a water cistern dug into the rock. On the upper level, check out the black stone slab bearing an inscription in Estrangelo, or East Syriac, brought by the founders of the Lebanese Maronite Order when they arrived from Aleppo.

Getting there and away There is a good road all the way to the monastery, which is the easiest (though longest) walking route there. Either walking or driving, head east out of Bcharre and follow the road as it loops round to head west along the south rim of the Qadisha Valley, passing the **River Roc** and **Mississippi** restaurant. After a little under 3 km there is a right turn (signposted 'Qadisha Valley' and 'Convent St Elisee') directly opposite the **Al-Reef** restaurant.

Immediately below the road on the way down is the monastery of Mar Elisha, which has replaced the much older monastery of the same name near the valley bottom, built into the rock face on the far (north) side of the valley. Follow the road all the way down; there are stunning views of the entire valley along the way.

If you're walking, you can diverge off the main road about halfway (one hour) down. There is a path signposted 'The Cross Path' on the right-hand side of the road, where you can follow a good trail all the way to the monastery.

Continuing along the main road, on the valley floor, by the stream, there are several seasonal cafés and restaurants. Just across the stream, a narrow surfaced road climbs steeply up to the original monastery. It takes approximately two hours to walk down to the monastery this way from Bcharre.

It is also possible to reach Deir Mar Elisha directly by heading down the steep valley side from Bcharre. The path is a little tricky in places, and unfortunately also takes you through some rather unsightly ad hoc rubbish tips.

Deir Qannoubin

The name Qannoubin is taken from the Greek Koinobion, meaning literally 'community' ('koinos' = common 'bios' = life). This is perhaps one of the oldest monasteries in the Qadisha Valley, founded according to some sources by Theodosius the Great in the late fourth century AD. According to Maronite legend, the Mamluk Sultan Barquq (1382-1399), having escaped from Kerak castle (in present-day Jordan) where he was imprisoned after being briefly deposed in 1389, came to the Qadisha Valley and stayed at Qannoubin, before going on to regain his Sultancy. Impressed by the hospitality he received and the way of life of the people there, he subsequently made substantial endowments, allowing the monastery to be restored after centuries of decay. From 1440 until 1790, Qannoubin was the permanent residence of the Maronite Patriarchs.

Today, Deir Qannoubin is a working convent run by Antonine sisters, and in its simplicity and isolated tranquillity (except perhaps on Sundays during the summer months, when it is generally busy with pilgrims) gives a genuine sense of the Maronite monastic/hermitic tradition, without any of the commercialization or crisp restoration to be found elsewhere.

The monastery's church, with its barrel-vaulted ceiling, is partly built into the cliff face. On one of the side walls there is a large fresco depicting 'Le Gloire de Marie' (the coronation of the Virgin Mary by the Trinity, witnessed by an assembly of Maronite Patriarchs). The lower parts of the fresco are peeling badly due to dampness, but the upper part is still clearly discernible. Below the fresco there is a small baptismal font set inside a recess. In the semi-domed apse behind the altar there is a fresco depicting Jesus flanked by the Virgin Mary and St Stephen (this being a variation on the traditional formulation of Jesus flanked by Mary and St John the Baptist, known as a *Deisis*), while two niches on either side depict St Joseph holding the baby Jesus and Daniel in the lion's den.

Just to the west of the monastery is the **Chapel of Mar Marina**, containing the tombs of the Maronite Patriarchs of Qannoubin. Born at Qalamoun, on the coast just south of Tripoli, St Marina is said to have disguised herself as a monk and lived her life as a hermit at Deir Qannoubin. Finding an abandoned baby, she saved it by breast-feeding it herself (much to the surprise of her fellow monks), and today mothers unable to produce breast milk make pilgrimages to Deir Qannoubin seeking her intervention. It is possible to continue up the side of the valley from here, along a very steep (and in places tricky) path, to arrive eventually in Blawza, but you are advised to take a local guide for this hike.

Getting there Returning to the valley floor from Deir Mar Elisha, you can follow a good track along the north bank of the Qadisha river, clearly signposted to Deir Qannoubin. Although it's possible to drive along it for all but the final couple of kilometres, it is much more rewarding to walk. The valley here is wooded and green, and carpeted with flowers during the spring, with terracing and cultivation wherever possible on the steep slopes, and waterfalls cascading down from the sheer cliffs above.

After around 1 km, steps on the left lead down to the stream, with a bridge across to a particularly beautiful and secluded restaurant with a terrace area shaded by vines (open only during the summer months). Around 2 km further on, the track forks; bear right here to keep to the upper level. A couple of kilometres further on, the track gives way to a concrete-covered irrigation channel (not wide enough for cars). Follow this, passing the tiny isolated hamlet of Qannoubine where there are a few houses and a simple restaurant, until you reach a clearly signposted path off to the right, leading steeply up to Deir Qannoubin. Allow at least one hour to walk here from Deir Mar Elisha, or more like 1½ to two hours if you want to take it slowly or stop along the way.

The south rim of the Qadisha Valley

Ins and outs
Getting there and away All the buses heading between Tripoli and Bcharre pass through the southern rim of the valley, and you can ask to be dropped at any point along the way.

Bqaa Kafra
At an altitude of 1750 m, this tiny village is the highest in Lebanon. Its main claim to fame, however, is as the birthplace of St Charbel (see page 78). The simple wood-beamed house where he was born has been converted into a small chapel, and around this has grown a small monastery, which includes a museum with contemporary paintings depicting scenes from his life, as well as statues and busts of the man. The annual feast of St Charbel is celebrated here on the third Sunday in July.

Getting there and away From Bcharre heading west on the main road running along the south rim of the Qadisha Valley, around 1.5 km beyond the turning down to Deir Mar Elisha you come to the village of Bqar Qacha. Here, a left turn is signposted to Bqaa Kafra, a steep 2-km climb up a narrow road that zig-zags its way up the mountainside.

Deir Mar Samaan (St Simon's hermitage)
Back on the main road, some 400 m past the turning for Bqaa Kafra (still in Bqar Qacha village), there is a small blue sign with white writing in Arabic indicating the start of a footpath leading off to the right, down to Deir Mar Samaan. This hermitage is believed to have been originally founded in 1112 by Takla, the daughter of a local priest and later inhabited by St Simon.

A concrete path and steps lead steeply down to the cave where St Simon lived as a hermit. The views down into the Qadisha Valley are spectacular. When you reach a concrete bell tower you can either continue down to a small shrine below the cave, or follow a narrow ledge and then climb via a metal ladder up into the cave itself. This involves crouching and squeezing through two tiny doorways cut into the rock and is only for the agile or determined. There are candles and offerings in the tiny and surprisingly exposed cave, as well as a book in which the faithful have written prayers. One can only wonder what it must have been like to live in such conditions through winters at this altitude.

Continuing along the main road, a short distance further on there is a cemetery off to the right of the road. A track leads round the side of the cemetery and down past a quarry to a rocky outcrop (in fact the top of the cliff in which St Simon's hermitage is located), from where there are even more spectacular views down into the Qadisha Valley.

Bazaoun and Hasroun

Around 1 km further along the main road you come to the twin villages of Bazaoun and Hasroun, some 5-6 km from the centre of Bcharre. Both villages, Hasroun in particular, are very picturesque, much more so than Bcharre. Here the old Ottoman-period buildings, with their distinctive old stonework, arched windows and pyramid-shaped red-tiled roofs still outnumber the modern concrete buildings. Away from the sometimes frenetic traffic along the main road, there is a relaxed, unhurried atmosphere about the place.

Bearing off to the right in the centre of Hasroun to head downhill, you come to the **church of the Virgin Mary** (Eglise Notre Dame). The church features a large clock tower with a dial giving the date in Arabic below the standard clock face, and a pretty bell tower to the right. In front of it is a fountain and statue of Josephus Simon Assemani, a 17th-century doctor from the village. Further down, you come to the tiny **church of St Jude** (Knisset Mar Leba), where you can take a series of steps that lead down into the plain, barrel-vaulted interior of undressed stone. A little further on, past a couple of modern buildings, there are further marvellous views into the Qadisha Valley, which drops away in a sheer cliff face from here.

Diman

Around 4 km beyond Bazaoun and Hasroun is the village of Diman. There is a large, imposing monastery and church here that today serves as the summer residence of the Maronite Patriarch (in winter he retreats to his main residence at Bkerke, above Jounieh). Dating from 1939, the monastery and church are not particularly beautiful and without a formal introduction you are unlikely to be allowed inside anyway. Just beyond Diman is the tiny village of **Brissat**, with a couple of snack and pizza places, as well as a small new church.

Hadath el-Jobbe

A couple of kilometres beyond Brissat you come to the village of Hadath el-Jobbe, 13 km from Bcharre. In the centre of the village there is a left turn opposite the police station (*gendarmerie*) which is the start of the road leading via the cedars of Arz Tannourine to Tannourine el-Faouqa, from where you can continue on to the ski resort of Laqlouq in Kesrouan region or to the town of Douma (see page 80).

Continuing straight along the main road, if you bear right where it forks near the village of Qnat, this route takes you back towards the coast via Amioun.

The north rim of the Qadisha Valley

Ins and outs

Getting there and away There's no regular public transport along the north rim of the valley; the best way to explore this area is with your own transport or hiring a taxi from Bcharre.

Hadchit

Heading west out of Bcharre to follow the north rim of the Qadisha Valley, you come first to the village of Hadchit (3 km). Although signposted on the main road, the heart of the old village is off to the left (south) of the road. On the way down to the village square you pass the **church of St Sarkis**, with part of a Roman column still standing outside. In the square itself is the **church of St Raymond**, with a Roman statue outside, minus its head and arms. Previously this stood inside the church, until it was condemned as a pagan idol and its head and arms smashed off before being removed.

The feast of St Raymond is celebrated each year in the village from the last Sunday in August to the first Sunday in September. Nearby is the smaller **church of the Virgin Mary**. A difficult path (you really need a local guide for this) descends steeply from Hadchit down to the grotto of **Deir es-Salib** (monastery of the cross), a tiny monastery built into caves in the side of the cliff face, although today in an advanced state of ruin. Deir es-Salib can also be reached by a path leading up from the track along the floor of the valley (see above), but again you really need a local guide to find it. There are the remains of numerous other hermitages, chapels and tiny monasteries in the immediate vicinity.

Blawza and Hawqa

Returning to the main road and continuing west, 2 km further on you pass through the village of Blawza. A path descends from Blawza to Dier Qannoubin, down in the Qadisha Valley (see above). A little over 1 km further on there is a left turn signposted for 'Hawka'. This road leads through the village of Hawqa, from where you can carry on down to the monastery of **Deir Mar Antonios Qozhaya** (5 km) on a winding, at times almost precarious, road with dramatic views down into the Qadisha Valley. The more commonly used approach to the monastery is via a turning off the main road beyond Ehden leading down towards Amioun. Note that it is not possible to do a loop, descending by one road and leaving by the other, as the monastery itself blocks access between the two roads. A steep footpath leads down from Hawqa to **Saydet Hawqa** (Our Lady of Hawqa), consisting of a small chapel and monks' cells built into a shallow cave. On 14 August each year a high mass is celebrated in the chapel, during the feast of the Assumption of the Virgin.

Bané and Kfar Sghab

Beyond the turning for Hawqa, the main road veers northeast, following a side valley that drains into the Qadisha Valley and passing through the villages of Bané and Kfar Sghab. Many of the inhabitants of these villages (along with those of Blawza and Hadchit) emigrated to Australia during the civil war, the majority of them settling in Sydney, and the Antipodean connection here remains strong. During the summer many of them return home to visit relatives, and many of the locals speak English with a thick Australian accent.

Ehden

The large village of Ehden is popular as a summer resort and famous for its springside restaurants up on the hillside to the northeast of the main town. The old village (at the east end of town) is quite picturesque, while extending to the west along the main road (which widens out to a two-lane affair) is some modern development. To the right of the main road as you enter the old village coming from Bcharre is a pleasant square with a fountain in the centre and a number of cafés and small restaurants, all thronging with people on summer evenings.

Ehden's other claim to fame is as the summer residence of the Franjieh family. The summer 'palace' of Suleiman Franjieh, president of Lebanon from 1970 to 1976, is near the roundabout at the far western end of town. Today it is occupied by his grandson, Robert Franjieh, his son Tony having been murdered in 1978 by gunmen of Gemayal's rival Phalange militia, along with his wife and daughter and 32 of his supporters.

Statue of Youssuf Bey Karam and St George's church Opposite the square in the centre of the old part of Ehden, a signpost points up to the statue of Youssuf (Joseph) Bey Karam (1823-1889), a Maronite hero of the struggle against Ottoman rule in Lebanon who drew wide support for his cause from the Greek Orthodox, Sunni and Shiite communities as well as fellow Maronites. Born in Ehden, he was finally defeated and driven into exile after leading rebellions against the Ottomans in 1864 and 1867. The statue, depicting him riding proudly into battle on horseback, stands in front of **St George's church**, in which there is a glass-topped mausoleum containing Karam's mummified body. Many of the families in this area bear the surname Karam, a clan that rose to importance in the region long before Joseph Bey Karam's time.

Saydet el-Hosn and St Mema High up on the hillside to the northwest of Ehden, dominating the skyline, is the large, modernistic church of Saydet el-Hosn (Our Lady of the Castle). Next to it, and completely dwarfed by it, is a much smaller and older church of the same name, which was probably originally built on the site of a Roman fortress (hence the name). Note the small face (said to be that of Jesus) carefully carved into a stone in one corner of the church exterior. On the way up to Saydet el-Hosn, you pass a **statue of Stephen Douweihy**, Maronite Patriarch from 1670-1704, who was responsible for many of the important reforms of the Maronite church during this period and who acquired a reputation for his piety and dedication. Another interesting church is that of St Mema, on the main road as you head out of Ehden towards Bcharre, which dates back to AD 749.

Horsh Ehden Nature Reserve ① *T06-660120, www.horshehden.org, daily 0800-1700, information centre and toilets are located at the main Aain al-Bayada entrance (just over 3 km from the village of Ehden itself, signposted from town).* Covering approximately 1000 ha of mountain terrain above Ehden, the Horsh Ehden Nature Reserve was established in 1991 by the Friends of Horsh Ehden in an attempt to preserve the area's unique natural forest habitat. Nearly half the reserve is forest-clad, with large stands of Lebanese cedars (accounting for 20% of Lebanon's remaining cedar forests), as well as some 39 other species of trees. Horsh Ehden is also home to a wide variety of mammals, including wolves, wildcats and striped hyenas, as well as weasels, badgers, hares, hedgehogs and porcupine. Birds to be seen here include the Imperial eagle, Bonnelli's eagle and the globally threatened cornrake. In all, more than 1000 species of plants have been identified here, of which more than 100 are endemic to Lebanon, while 10 are endemic to the reserve.

Several marked hiking trails have been established through the reserve's often dramatically beautiful scenery. **Trail 8** begins at the Aain al-Bayada entrance and is an easy, flat walk with excellent views over the valley. It ends at Aain al-Na'asa spring from where you can continue walking on several other trails that showcase the diverse vegetation of the reserve.

Deir Mar Antonios Qozhaya
Built into the side of a cliff face in the same way as Deir Mar Elisha, this is one of the largest monasteries in the Qadisha Valley. First founded as a monastery in the 10th or 11th century, it is famous for having established the first known printing press in the Middle East, during the late 16th century. Today the monastery is a popular pilgrimage site, though somewhat commercialized and lacking entirely the sense of isolation found at Qannoubin.

Built up against the cliff face along one side of a large courtyard is the façade of the **church**. Its doorway is beautifully decorated with alternating bands of stone and intricate carved patterns. Above is a long row of small arched windows, again intricately decorated, and a triple bell tower. Inside, the vaulted stonework of the church blends in with the natural rock of the cave behind. By the entrance to the main courtyard and church there is a large cave, the **grotto of St Anthony**, where you can see the chains and shackles used to restrain the insane, who were brought here in the belief that they would be cured by the saint.

Below the courtyard and church there is a large souvenir shop selling all sorts of tacky religious souvenirs. This leads through to a **museum** displaying a number of old manuscripts (including a Syriac-Arabic dictionary dating from 1702 and a Latin-Arabic dictionary dating from 1639), various sacred relics and items of religious paraphernalia, and a printing press imported from Edinburgh (although itself dating from 1609, this press was only purchased during the 19th century, replacing earlier ones).

Getting there and away From Ehden, head west along the main road; 2 km beyond the roundabout at the west end of town, you come to a left turn (marked by a statue of St Charbel in the centre of the junction), the start of the road leading down towards the coast via Amioun. Taking this left turn, after just under 4 km you come to a left turn signposted for 'Couvent St Antoine Kosbaiya'; take this turn to get to Deir Mar Antonios Qozhaya (Monastery of St Anthony Qozhaya).

The Cedars (Al Arz)

When the French established an army skiing school here in the 1930s, The Cedars became the first of Lebanon's ski resorts. Today it is the second most popular ski resort after Mzaar and although not as developed, its higher altitude (maximum 2800 m) means that the season generally runs for slightly longer (mid-November to late April). Just out of town is the famous cedar stand, known locally as *Al Arz al-Rab* (The Cedars of the Lord), from which the resort takes its name. This small stand of around 300 cedars is all that remains of the once extensive cedar forests that covered this landscape.

During the ski season, especially on weekends, The Cedars gets extremely busy. In summer this tiny village is a sleepy, near dormant, destination during the week, though weekends see the resort slightly busier with local hotels awakening to The Cedars action-adventure potential. Many now offer mountain bikes and ATVs for hire, and this is also one of the main locations in Lebanon where you can learn to paraglide during the summer.

Ins and outs
Getting there Except during the ski season, when you may find a service taxi heading up here from Bcharre, there is no public transport to The Cedars. A private taxi from Bcharre costs around 10,000 LBP.

If you're driving, there are two roads from Bcharre. Following the road up out of town, signposted 'The Cedars', you can either keep going straight along the new road or turn sharp right (signposted 'Qadisha Grotto') to go via the **L'Aiglion Hotel** and the grotto. Both roads join up at the top of the plateau and lead to the ski resort (8 km from Bcharre). Further up, beyond the ski resort, is the stand of cedars itself.

Skiing at The Cedars
ⓘ *Mon-Fri 0800-1530, Sat-Sun 0800-1600, weekdays US$23, under 16-years US$20, weekends US$30, under 16-years US$20, weekdays half-day pass (after 1200) US$17, weekends half-day pass (after 1200) US$23.*

The excellent slopes and high quality of the snow have given The Cedars something of a reputation as a resort for 'serious' skiers. However, this is also a good all-round destination for skiers and snowboarders of all levels, with excellent cross-country skiing available here and a variety of gentle slopes for complete beginners to practise on.

As well as the main **Pic de Dames** chairlift, which reaches 2800 m, there are three ski lifts and four baby lifts. A gondola is also being constructed at the slopes which, when finished, will be able to transport skiers and visitors from the ski station up to the highest accessible summit at 2870 m. Ski equipment is available for hire from a number of the hotels from around US$5-12 per day, while, as well as renting and selling ski equipment, the **Tony Arida Centre** has its own skiing school with professional instructors. There is a duty doctor at the resort during the season and Red Cross teams in attendance on weekends. The main road up to the resort (via Amioun, Hadath el-Jobbe and Bcharre) is kept open throughout the season.

The cedar trees

ⓘ *Daily summer 0900-1800, winter 0900-1600, by donation (5000 LBP per person is appropriate).*
Today all that remains of the once extensive forests that gave the area its name is a small, somewhat forlorn stand of around 300 cedars in a landscape otherwise practically bereft of any trees. Although at first sight something of a disappointment, this stand nevertheless contains some of the oldest and largest cedar trees in Lebanon, rising to a height of 35 m and estimated to be between 1000-1500 (or by some accounts up to 2000) years old.

The steady depletion of Mount Lebanon's cedar forests has taken place over thousands of years, but it was only by the mid-19th century it began to dawn on the local people that they would soon disappear altogether. The Maronite Patriarchs of Bcharre placed them under their personal protection, building a small chapel in the midst of the stand in 1843 and forbidding any further felling of the trees. In 1876 Queen Victoria financed the building of a protective wall around the cedars, important for keeping out grazing goats.

Today, the **Friends of the Cedars' Committee** at Bcharre has taken over responsibility for protecting them, repairing the enclosure wall and marking out a path through the trees. In addition, there are various projects in place to carry out further research into the trees and to plant new stands in the surrounding areas. There are numerous souvenir shops around the entrance to the enclosure selling all kinds of cedar wood trinkets (carved from naturally fallen timber only), as well as a number of cafés and snack places.

Qornet es-Saouda

It is perhaps typical of the car-obsessed Lebanese that they should have built a motorable track to the summit of their highest mountain. For hikers there are a number of other routes to the summit, ask in Bcharre or The Cedars for a guide.

After around 7 km following the main road along from the stand of cedar trees, a narrow side road (marked by a large overhead sign with Arabic writing and Coca Cola logos) branches off to the left at a point where the main road hairpins sharply round to the right. Taking this side road, after 2.5 km a rough jeep track branches off to the left. This jeep track climbs up to the summit of Qornet es-Saouda (3083 m). In summer it is passable in a 4WD almost all the way.

The Cedars to the Bekaa Valley

From The Cedars a road continues up the mountainside, crosses the high ridges of the Lebanon mountain range and descends into the Bekaa Valley beyond, before arriving in Baalbek. Check that it is open before you attempt it – from around late October to late May it is usually blocked by snow. Once open, the road is reasonably good, though pot-holed in places, particularly on the far side.

Take the main road continuing past the cedar tree stand and past the turning for Qornet es-Saouda. After another couple of kilometres of climbing you reach the watershed of the Lebanon mountain range. The road then descends, through numerous hairpin bends, down to **Ainata** (15 km from the summit), a small village with a couple of simple restaurants offering snacks and tea/coffee, etc. Leaving Ainata, you pass through an army checkpoint, and then 3 km beyond this there is a sharp right turn for Yammouné. Continuing straight on, you pass through a couple of tiny villages, and then through the sprawling village of **Deir al-Ahmar** overlooking the flat plain of the Bekaa. After a further 5 km, fork left for Baalbek (signposted). Follow this road across the flat plain, going straight over a crossroads (15 km from Deir el-Ahmar; right for Zahle), to arrive in the centre of Baalbek.

Qadisha Valley and The Cedars listings

For Sleeping and Eating price codes and other relevant information, see pages 9-10.

🛏 Sleeping

Bcharre *p86*
Bcharre is an excellent base for budget travellers due to the dorm accommodation available. There are only 3 hotels in the village – 1 budget and 2 mid-range, and outside the peak summer and peak ski seasons it's nearly always possible to negotiate discounts at the mid-range hotels. Note that none of the hotels provide fan or a/c but all have heating in the winter.
$$ Chbat, Rue Gibran, T06-671270, www. hotelchbat.com. This old-style, family-run hotel is bursting with character. Up a rabbit warren of staircases are a variety of rooms. All are large, clean and boast a hodge-podge of dated furniture and satellite TV and some of the better ones also have separate lounge areas and splendid views over the valley. The bathrooms could all do with an update, but are perfectly serviceable. If you're on the tall side you might want to check a few before deciding, as some of the showers are ridiculously short. This is a solid and homely

choice run by the ultra-friendly Wadih Chbat (a mine of information on the area). Restaurants, swimming pool, parking, bar, breakfast included, Wi-Fi.
$$-$ Palace, main road (Rue Antoine Choueiri), T06-671460, www.palace hotelbsharry.com. This cheerfully colourful hotel is slap in the centre of town. Undergoing extensive restoration work when we visited, the rooms here should have all benefited from a bright lick of paint and some bathroom renovations by the time you visit. The cheaper rooms in the atmospheric older wing are all large and bright with good-sized bathrooms and simple furnishings. More expensive rooms in the new wing come with snazzy new bathroom fittings and furnishings, satellite TV and some have their own private balconies. The enthusiastic manager Charbel is a bundle of energy and is planning to set up a whole host of trekking and eco-tourism tours in the area. Breakfast included, Wi-Fi.
$ Tiger House, on the road to The Cedars, T06-672480, tigerhousepension@hotmail. com. Based in an extension of a family home, the ramshackle and extremely basic dorm rooms here (US$10) are a tad on

the small side, but who's complaining at this price. If you don't feel like sharing, for a little extra the dorm becomes a private single/double room. All rooms share clean bathrooms and surround a small common area (with TV). Laundry is available, the restaurant/café out front can rustle up a decent meal, and breakfast is an extra 5000 LBP. An excellent option for those on a budget. If you're coming by public transport let the bus driver know you're staying at Tiger House and he'll drop you right outside the door, saving you the uphill hike from the town square. Recommended.

Bazaoun and Hasroun *p91*
$$ Karam, main road, on the left (coming from Bcharre), T06-591189. A friendly hotel in a lovely old building offering simple but clean rooms all with good modern bathrooms and balcony. There's a decent restaurant serving up Lebanese specialities.
$ Palace, main road, on left heading west, towards the outskirts of the village (there's no sign, so ask), T06-590115. Open May-Nov. A family-run hotel occupying a beautiful old building with a large garden at the rear and terrace out front. Simple rooms all come with balcony. Great value and a real homely feel.

Ehden *p92*
Outside the peak summer season (approx Jul-Sep) discounts can usually be negotiated.
$$$ Grand Hotel Abchi, above main road towards west end of town (it's impossible to miss), T06-561101. This large, imposing building with its bizarre UFO-shaped restaurant has comfortable rooms all with satellite TV and balcony that provide stunning views. Swimming pool.
$$$ Masters, approx 2 km above Ehden (clearly signposted from the roundabout at the west end of town), T06-561052. This hotel's best point is the superb views – all the way down to Tripoli and the Mediterranean, and north to Syria – you

have from your private balcony. The rooms here are pleasantly furnished and come with satellite TV. Restaurant, bar, breakfast included.
$$ Belmont, near roundabout at west end of town, T06-560102. A friendly hotel with great staff offering decent, if a bit bland, rooms (some with balcony). Breakfast included.
$$ La Reserve, entrance to Horsh Ehden Reserve, T06-561092, www. lareservehorshehden.com. Cute little wooden chalets right beside the reserve's entrance, so great for hikers, birdwatchers and other nature lovers. Open summer only, when the owners can also organize a whole range of guided hikes and other activities within the reserve.

The Cedars (Al Arz) *p94*
Price categories are for the winter skiing season; outside of this period expect substantial discounts. Most hotels are extremely open to bargaining outside peak season. Note that many of the hotels offer apartments that come with kitchenettes and some can sleep up to 10 or so people, making them excellent value if you are travelling with a group of friends. Others offer the option of ski packages that include full/half board as well, which can work out cheaper than just booking the room. All hotels below have heating in the rooms.
$$$$ L'Auberge des Cedres, take the right-hand turn after the Alpine Hotel and follow the signposts, T06-678888, T03-566953, www.smresorts.net. Away from the main road, this resort looks for all the world like it has been transported directly from the Swiss Alps with its beautiful wood facade all covered in vines. Inside, lovely old *kilims* and carpets cover the floors and add a local feel to the otherwise traditional county-lodge decoration with lots of dark wood and quaint old-worldy touches to make the rooms feel cosy. During summer months guests can also stay in their new luxury tents. The staff here are ultra friendly and

can help arrange all sorts of activities.

$$$$-$$$ Toni Arida Centre, main road, T06-678195, T03-321998, habibarida@ yahoo.com. This is a 1-stop shop for skiers and snowboarders, owned and run by Toni Arida, Lebanon's first qualified ski instructor and quite a character. With ski shop and ski rental, a ski school and access to their own baby-lift/beginners' slopes, as well as a restaurant and nightclub, the centre has all bases covered. There's a selection of cosy apartments here that all come with lounge (satellite TV, open fire), kitchenette and some severely dated furnishings. The larger (and more expensive) ones can sleep up to 8. Good value for groups, though rather overpriced for couples. Good discounts are available out of ski season.

$$$ Le Cedrus, main road, T06-678777, www.cedrushotel.com. Unfortunately the plush interior of the reception doesn't quite follow through to the rooms which, though large and comfortable (satellite TV), could do with the bathrooms being updated. Management are friendly and helpful, there's free Wi-Fi and the excellent Le Pichot restaurant is below. Breakfast included.

$$$-$$ Mon Refuge, main road, T03-734312. A homely place with welcoming staff and management. There's a choice of apartments, which can sleep up to 7, or good-value rooms which make a decent mid-range option for doubles and singles. A bit on the small side, the low-ceilinged rooms come with little terraces and are bright and clean. There's a restaurant and bar downstairs and if you're feeling like a boogie staff are keen to switch on the hilarious disco lights and get the party started. Outside peak season (and on weekdays during the season) management are open to bargaining. Wi-Fi, breakfast included.

$$$-$$ Alpine, main road, T03-213102, elie2@hotmail.com. This hotel has a large homely lounge downstairs with a roomy bar and games room as well as a lovely outdoor terrace. Upstairs there are a

selection of large, bright and comfortable rooms (satellite TV) that all have spacious bathrooms and small balconies. The more expensive ones come with magnificent views.

$ Auberge Ecoclub Bcharre, main road, T06-678999. On the road between Bcharre and The Cedars, the Auberge has cheap and cheerful dorm beds on offer, which make it a nice option if you have your own transport. It was being renovated at the time of research so couldn't be visited, so ring to check it's open again before turning up. Member of the DHIAFEE hotel network.

🍴 Eating

Bcharre *p86*

If you've got your own transport there are a number of restaurants along the road leading from Bcharre along the southern rim of the Qadisha Valley towards Bazraoun/Hasroun. Some of the closer ones have been included below.

There are some great cheap options in Bcharre. One of the best stocked supermarkets in town is the **Kangaroo** supermarket on the main road. Right beside it is a tiny basic falafel store, where you can get a filling falafel sandwich for 2000 LBP. On the stairs to the right of the town square there is a popular café with a few tables outside which does a range of sandwiches for 1500-3000 LBP, and there are numerous *mannoushi* places around town. The **Manakish** on the main road is one pick, but there are 4 or 5 others as well.

†† Al-Reef, approx 3 km past the waterfall, directly opposite the road turning down to the Qadisha Valley floor. This delightfully friendly option may not have any views (it's on the wrong side of the road) but it does really super Lebanese cuisine and is a fantastic option if you have your own transport.

†† Le Montagnard, under the Chbat Hotel, on the road leading up to The Cedars. A great option in town, with a menu that should have something for everyone; pizzas, pasta, crêpes, sandwiches, salads, burgers and soups are all here. If you fancy some typical Lebanese home cooking, the hotel's other restaurant (upstairs) is a good choice.

♔ River Roc, approx 1 km past the waterfall. A pleasant and well-run place serving up excellent Lebanese cuisine with helpful staff and an outdoor terrace with incredible views.

♔ RTC, right on the junction, on the road leading up to The Cedars. A rather trendy café/bar that serves up some decent international favourites and also has a great outdoor terrace, a good place to hang out with a beer in the evening.

♕ Al-Dayaa, main square. A cheap and cheerful option smack in the centre of town. Always popular with locals, the Al-Dayaa dishes up all the usual Lebanese staples.

♕ Pizza Les Copains, beside the Coral petrol station, close to the waterfall, main road. This little place does a decent pizza with seating out on a small covered terrace.

Bazaoun and Hasroun *p91*

As well as the restaurant below the Karam Hotel, there are several cafés and simple snack places along or just off the main road through Bazaoun and Hasroun.

Ehden *p92*

To reach Ehden's famous spring-side restaurants (open in summer only), take the turning opposite the small church of St Mema and bear right around 200 m further on, at a mini-roundabout with a church beside it. Follow this road for around 1.5 km to the point where the Nebaa Mar Sarkis spring emerges from the hillside. Here there are a group of restaurants all specializing in Lebanese cuisine, in particular lavish meze spreads, often with live entertainment on summer evenings.

In town itself there are several cafés/restaurants around the lively main square which are great places for a simple meal or a quick snack.

The Cedars (Al Arz) *p94*

As well as the hotel restaurants, there are several snack bars and restaurants at the entry to the cedar forest itself, open all year round. There are also a few places near the foot of the slopes, although most of them are only open during the skiing season.

♔♔ Le Pichot, main road. The top restaurant here, with a menu that leans towards Italian but also covers a range of Lebanese and other international dishes. Mains average about 20,000 LBP, but if you stick to the meze or the range of pizzas and pastas (13,000-18,000 LBP), meals are considerably cheaper. The signature Le Pichot pizza (mozzarella, rocca, parmesan and ham) is particularly delicious.

♔ La Tombe La Neige, main road. A narrow little bar/restaurant right in the centre of town with a French-inspired menu. The nachos are tasty and there's a decent selection of soups and salads.

♔ Mon Refuge, Mon Refuge Hotel, main road. This is a cosy restaurant serving up hearty home cooking at decent prices. Pizzas, pasta and burgers and a great selection of grills.

▲ Activities and tours

The Qadisha Valley has excellent hiking potential with **Bcharre**, **Ehden** and **The Cedars** being the 3 obvious bases from which to head out. Ehden is the starting point for section 6 of the Lebanon Mountain Trail (LMT), which heads into the Qadisha Valley passing by several of the valley's monasteries before finishing in the hamlet of Qannoubine, where one of the valley's most famous monasteries can be visited. Section 7 then heads from Qannoubine to Bcharre. Both these trails are extremely worthwhile and are fairly easy to walk yourself, though hiring a local guide for the day can add a lot to your entire trail experience. For further information on the LMT go to www.lebanontrail.org.

There are literally dozens of other hikes within the Qadisha Valley and many of the lesser known trails are difficult to find without a guide. 2 experienced local guides: **Georges Zougeib**, T70-105546. **Joe Rahme**, T06-678999.

Several of the Beirut-based hiking clubs such as **Vamos Todos** (www.vamos-todos. com), **Esprit Nomade** (www.esprit-nomade. com) and **Liban Trek** (www.libantrek.com) regularly run weekend/day trips to the Qadisha Valley, a great way to hike in this area if you're a solo traveller.

⊖ Transport

Bcharre *p86*
Buses to **Tripoli** (1¼ hr, 4000 LBP), leave from the main square approx every 30 mins from 0800-1200 and every hour afterwards until nightfall. Service taxis also congregate in the square as well, but departures aren't as frequent. They travel via the southern rim of the Qadisha Valley. There's no regular public transport to The Cedars or along the northern rim of the Qadisha Valley. A private taxi to **The Cedars** or **Ehden** will cost about 10,000 LBP. If you want to hire a taxi to Baalbek from here, it will cost about US$50.

❶ Directory

Bcharre *p86*
Banks The BLC Bank is on the main road near the waterfall and there is also an exchange office, the **Tawk Exchange,** further along the road. **Internet** 2 internet cafés on the main road in the centre of Bcharre. **Medical services** Along the main road; the **Pharmacy St George** and **Pharmacy Simona. Telephone** Card-phones along the main road in town.

Contents

Foontoes

Index

Titles available in the Footprint *Focus* range

Latin America	UK RRP	US RRP
Bahia & Salvador	£7.99	$11.95
Buenos Aires & Pampas	£7.99	$11.95
Costa Rica	£8.99	$12.95
Cuzco, La Paz & Lake Titicaca	£8.99	$12.95
El Salvador	£5.99	$8.95
Guadalajara & Pacific Coast	£6.99	$9.95
Guatemala	£8.99	$12.95
Guyana, Guyane & Suriname	£5.99	$8.95
Havana	£6.99	$9.95
Honduras	£7.99	$11.95
Nicaragua	£7.99	$11.95
Paraguay	£5.99	$8.95
Quito & Galápagos Islands	£7.99	$11.95
Recife & Northeast Brazil	£7.99	$11.95
Rio de Janeiro	£8.99	$12.95
São Paulo	£5.99	$8.95
Uruguay	£6.99	$9.95
Venezuela	£8.99	$12.95
Yucatán Peninsula	£6.99	$9.95

Asia	UK RRP	US RRP
Angkor Wat	£5.99	$8.95
Bali & Lombok	£8.99	$12.95
Chennai & Tamil Nadu	£8.99	$12.95
Chiang Mai & Northern Thailand	£7.99	$11.95
Goa	£6.99	$9.95
Hanoi & Northern Vietnam	£8.99	$12.95
Ho Chi Minh City & Mekong Delta	£7.99	$11.95
Java	£7.99	$11.95
Kerala	£7.99	$11.95
Kolkata & West Bengal	£5.99	$8.95
Mumbai & Gujarat	£8.99	$12.95

Africa	UK RRP	US RRP
Beirut	£6.99	$9.95
Damascus	£5.99	$8.95
Durban & KwaZulu Natal	£8.99	$12.95
Fès & Northern Morocco	£8.99	$12.95
Jerusalem	£8.99	$12.95
Johannesburg & Kruger National Park	£7.99	$11.95
Kenya's beaches	£8.99	$12.95
Kilimanjaro & Northern Tanzania	£8.99	$12.95
Zanzibar & Pemba	£7.99	$11.95

Europe	UK RRP	US RRP
Bilbao & Basque Region	£6.99	$9.95
Granada & Sierra Nevada	£6.99	$9.95
Málaga	£5.99	$8.95
Orkney & Shetland Islands	£5.99	$8.95
Skye & Outer Hebrides	£6.99	$9.95

North America	UK RRP	US RRP
Vancouver & Rockies	£8.99	$12.95

Australasia	UK RRP	US RRP
Brisbane & Queensland	£8.99	$12.95
Perth	£7.99	$11.95

For the latest books, e-books and smart phone app releases, and a wealth of travel information, visit us at: www.footprinttravelguides.com.

footprinttravelguides.com

Join us on facebook for the latest travel news, product releases, offers and amazing competitions: www.facebook.com/footprintbooks.com.